GAY
POWER!

THE STONEWALL RIOTS
AND THE GAY RIGHTS MOVEMENT, 1969

BETSY **KUHN**

 TWENTY-FIRST CENTURY BOOKS ■ **MINNEAPOLIS**

The author would like to thank Urvashi Vaid, Jody West, Nancy Garden, and the staff of the Poolesville Library for their valuable and most welcome assistance.

Author's note: Imagine rooting in the attic through boxes of old family photographs and memorabilia. You come across a packet of papers from a relative—a great-uncle—you've never even heard about. As you sort through his letters and photographs, you uncover fascinating stories. You learn how, in the name of equal rights, he picketed the White House, stood up to hate, and faced down a whole police unit, despite the threat of losing his job and his home. Later you ask your mom, "Why didn't you ever tell me about this uncle?" She answers, "Well, you know, he was gay. We didn't think you'd be interested."

Not interested?! Not interested in hearing an amazing story of his courageous fight for equal rights? Are you kidding?

That's how I felt when I researched the Stonewall riots and the history of the LGBTQ movement. I wondered, "How is it that every American does not know this story?" Gay rights history has been almost entirely left out of mainstream U.S. history books. That's wrong. These stories are part of our nation's continual struggle to live up to the ideals set forth in the Declaration of Independence and the U.S. Constitution: equal rights for every citizen.

In writing any nonfiction book, the hardest part is having to leave out good material. That was especially true for this book; you can fit only so much history into 144 pages. So consider this book an introduction to LGBTQ history. I recommend you seek out books listed in the Further Reading section. You will be rewarded with inspiring and sometimes unbelievable stories.

Copyright © 2011 by Betsy Kuhn

Twenty-First Century Books
A division of Lerner Publishing Group, Inc.
241 First Avenue North
Minneapolis, MN 55401 U.S.A.

Website address: www.lernerbooks.com

Library of Congress Cataloging-in-Publication Data

Kuhn, Betsy.
    Gay power! : the Stonewall Riots and the gay rights movement, 1969 / by Betsy Kuhn.
      p.   cm. — (Civil rights struggles around the world)
    Includes bibliographical references and index.
    ISBN 978–0–7613–5768–1 (lib. bdg. : alk. paper)
     1. Stonewall Riots, New York, N.Y., 1969. 2. Gay liberation movement—United States—History.
   3. Gay rights—United States—History. I. Title.
   HQ76.8.U5K86 2011
   306.76′60973—dc22   2010028883

Manufactured in the United States of America
1 – CG – 12/31/10

CONTENTS

"POLICE! WE'RE TAKING THE PLACE!"

It was a busy night at the Stonewall Inn in Greenwich Village, a New York City neighborhood. On this night, June 28, 1969, the bar's jukebox was cranked. Couples jammed the dance floor, grooving to Stevie Wonder, the Stones, and the Supremes. In fact, many of the patrons had come primarily to dance. The Stonewall was one of the few places in all of New York City where they could dance the way they wanted: with members of their own sex. The Stonewall Inn was a gay bar. Its customers were mostly gay men, though it drew a few lesbians as well. In 1969 in New York, it was illegal for men to dance with men. But the Mafia, a criminal organization, ran the Stonewall along with most of the other gay bars in the city. The Mafia paid off the police, who agreed not to arrest the bar's customers. In return, the Stonewall's clientele had to live by the Mafia's rules. That meant paying too much for their watered-down drinks and enduring the Mafia's contempt. The reality of Mafia-run gay bars was just one of many unhappy facts of life for gay men and lesbians in 1969.

At least at the Stonewall, gay people could be themselves. In this dark little bar on Christopher Street, no one told them they were deviates, no psychiatrists told them they were sick, and no one threatened to hurt them because they were gay. Of course, there was always the threat of a police raid. Police had been raiding gay bars for decades.

The raids always unfolded the same way: The police barged into the bar, and the lights snap on. Officers checked the customers for identification, arrested the staff, and carted off the liquor. After that, the customers slipped away as quickly as possible into the night. Above all, they did not want their identities as gay men or lesbians exposed. Exposure could be disastrous. It was common and legal during this era for employers to fire people who were gay and for landlords to evict them. Many families rejected their own gay children.

Throughout June 1969, the city's police had raided a slew of gay bars, including the Stonewall. Gay people were getting fed up. In fact, they were getting fed up with a lot of the bad treatment they endured. So far, though, few gays and lesbians had been willing to risk exposing their sexuality to work for change.

At 1:28 A.M. on June 28, the police barged into the Stonewall. It was the second raid in a week. Officers stormed the place, locked the doors, tore up the furniture, and began lining up customers. On that night, though, the customers did not slink off into the darkness. On that night, they stayed, gathering outside the Stonewall Inn. These raids—and the horrible treatment of gay people—had to stop.

When the crowd saw the police shove a transvestite (a man dressed in women's clothing) into a patrol wagon, their anger boiled over. They began throwing pennies, then bottles and cans, at the police. They beat on the patrol wagon, and someone threw a cobblestone. It landed smack on the hood of a squad car.

The police were alarmed. Gay people fighting back? That almost never happened. Yet here the crowd was fired up and violent. The officers had to retreat into the Stonewall for safety while the crowd outside threw bricks, cobblestones, and even makeshift bombs at the inn.

Angry shouts filled the air. One shout rose above all the others: "Gay Power!"

The chant caught on. It was the beginning of a new era in gay and lesbian history.

CHAPTER 1

ALL THE PAST

HOMOSEXUALITY IN EARLY AMERICA

Then turn, and be not alarm'd
O Libertad—turn your undying face,
To where the future,
    greater than all the past,
Is swiftly, surely preparing for you."

—"Turn, O Libertad," poet Walt Whitman, *Leaves of Grass*, 1871–1872

■ In a scene in the HBO series *The Sopranos*, teenage AJ discusses the book *Billy Budd* with his big sister, Meadow. When Meadow points out that the book, which Herman Melville wrote in the 1800s, has a homosexual theme, AJ is taken aback. "I didn't know they had [gays] back then," he replies.

AJ's confusion is understandable. History has not told the full story. Prior to the Stonewall riots, few gay men and lesbians were willing to "come out of the closet"—that is, be open about their sexuality. Until then, an intimidating array of forces—legal and social—made coming out almost unthinkable.

Organized religions traditionally have considered homosexuality a sin, and for hundreds of years, governments treated same-sex relationships as a crime. In the mid-twentieth century, psychiatrists deemed homosexuality a mental illness.

What's more, the story of gays and lesbians in the United States is almost totally missing from history books, except for those that focus specifically on gay history. But whether their history is well known or not, gays and lesbians have been part of every human society, including early America.

"HERE SINCE THE BEGINNING"

Gays and lesbians "have been here since the beginning of the history of people," writes Larry Kramer, a leading gay activist.

Consider a few examples from American history. When army officers Meriwether Lewis and William Clark explored the North American West in 1806, Indians in Oregon directed them to a place where two young Indian men lived together. The men had left their tribe to make a home with each other. Some biographers think that Abraham Lincoln, who served as U.S. president from 1861 to 1865, had a gay relationship. "Boston marriages" were common in the late nineteenth and early twentieth century. In these relationships, two women lived together for long periods. We do not know if the relationships were sexual or not, but often they were romantic in nature. In many cases, the two women were well educated and

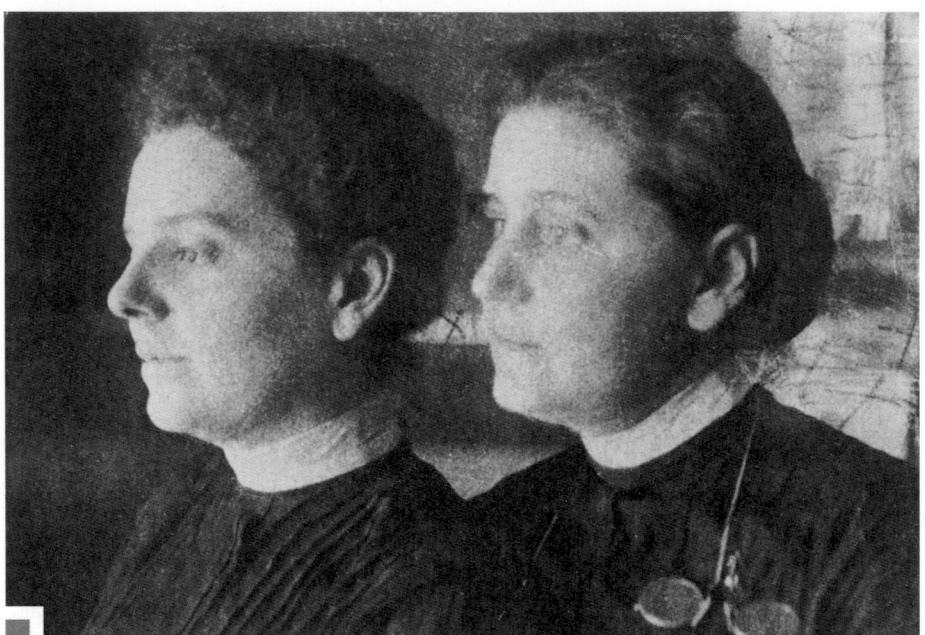

Jane Addams *(left)* **and Mary Rozet Smith** *(right)* **lived together in Illinois for many years in the late 1800s and early 1900s. Historians believe they were in a romantic relationship.**

well off. Because they had money, they could live independently rather than marry men. Jane Addams, a social reformer and peace activist, lived with a woman named Mary Rozet Smith for decades. Historians believe the two women were lesbians.

Most experts on Walt Whitman, a famous U.S. poet, believe that he was gay or bisexual. (Bisexuals are sexually attracted to members of their own sex as well as members of the opposite sex.) Whitman forged a number of extremely close relationships with other men.

Before Whitman died in March 1892, he might have followed a sensational story in that year's newspapers. In an article titled "A Most Shocking Crime," the *New York Times* reported that nineteen-year-old Alice Mitchell had attacked Freda Ward while Ward was riding in a carriage with her sister in Memphis, Tennessee. "Grasping Miss Ward by the neck, [Mitchell] drew a bright razor from out of the folds of her dress and without a word drew it across the throat of her victim," reported the *Times*. Ward died almost instantly.

"I killed Freda because I loved her," Mitchell later explained, "and she refused to marry me." A lawyer reported that Mitchell had once contacted him to ask if a woman could legally marry another woman. A doctor who met with Mitchell during her trial reported, "There was a mutual love between them such as between a male and female."

> **"Addie Phillips and Minnie Hubbard are each seventeen years of age. On Sunday the two girls disappeared and were not found for three days. Miss Phillips, on her return home, said that she loved Minnie and would rather be dead than separated from her. She further declared that she intended to marry her as soon as she secured some money."**
>
> —*Washington Post*, 1892

■ ■ ■ ■ "GOING AFTER STRANGE FLESH"

Just as gays and lesbians were part of early American history, so were laws that condemned homosexuality. Puritans, members of an English religious group, were some of the first European settlers in North America. In their new home, the Massachusetts Bay Colony, Puritans strived to please God and prosper. They feared they would perish if they angered God.

In 1641 the Massachusetts Puritans created the Body of Laws, the first legal code adopted by European settlers in the Americas. In some ways, the Body of Laws was quite progressive for its time. Unlike other law codes of the era, it forbade a man to beat his wife, "unless it be in his owne defence upon her assalt." The Body of Laws even spelled out rights for children and servants, who were usually without any.

The Body of Laws also spelled out twelve capital crimes, or crimes punishable by death. The law said, "If any man lyeth with mankinde as

This illustration shows a Puritan wedding in the 1600s. Puritans, some of the first European settlers in North America, wrote the Body of Laws. One of the laws made homosexuality illegal and punishable by death.

he lyeth with a woeman, both of them have committed abhomination, they both shall surely be put to death." The law used the words of the Old Testament, part of the Bible.

Eventually, every colony in North America had some sort of law against homosexuality. In 1655 the New Haven Colony outlawed "the going after strange flesh." The Rhode Island Colony condemned homosexuality as "a vile affection."

The only colony that did not impose the death penalty for homosexuality was Pennsylvania, which was home to a religious group called Quakers. Quakers opposed war and violence and called for the death penalty only in cases of murder. Pennsylvania law in the 1600s said that "such persons [homosexuals] shall be whipt"[1] and serve six months of hard labor. Later, under British rule, even Pennsylvania adopted laws that required the death penalty for homosexual activity.

By the time of the American Revolution (1775–1783), homosexuality was punishable by death in all thirteen colonies. After achieving independence from Great Britain, the United States retained laws against homosexuality. Rhode Island's law was typical. Under the state's Public Laws of 1798, "every person who shall be convicted of [homosexuality] . . . shall, for the first offence, be carried to . . . the common gaol [jail] there to be confined for a term not exceeding three years." For a second offense, the punishment was death.

Some states did execute people under antihomosexuality laws in the 1800s. Later in the century, all states changed their laws, replacing the death penalty for homosexuals with imprisonment and fines.

■ A HOMOSEXUAL IDENTITY

If you had asked a man in, say, 1865 if he were a homosexual, he would have responded with a blank stare. The term homosexual had yet to be coined. And gay meant "happy" or "carefree."

Enter journalist Karl Maria Kertbeny, born in Austria in 1824. As a young man, he lived in Germany, then part of the Prussian Empire. One of Kertbeny's close friends in Germany committed suicide. Kertbeny was dismayed to learn that the friend had killed himself after someone threatened to expose his terrible secret: the friend had had sex with other men, a crime in Prussia.

Kertbeny thought it was wrong that private sex between two willing parties should be a crime. If such acts were legal, he believed, his friend would still be alive. Kertbeny published two pamphlets calling for repeal of Prussia's laws against homosexuality. In these pamphlets, released in the late 1860s, he was the first person to use the term homosexual. He also coined the term heterosexual to refer to people who were sexually attracted to those of the opposite sex. The terms come from the Greek words for "same" (homos) and "different" (heteros).

Soon other writers began to use the term homosexual in their own work. When Sigmund Freud, the famed Austrian psychiatrist and father of psychoanalysis, used the term in his popular books and talks, it came into much wider use.

British doctor Havelock Ellis wrote a book in the late 1800s about gay men. He became sympathetic to the plight of gay people in a society that condemned them.

In the late nineteenth century, a small number of sexologists (people who study human sexuality) began to study homosexuality. They included Havelock Ellis, a British doctor. He began interviewing gay men in an effort to understand them. His book, *Sexual Inversion*, published in 1896, reported his findings. (*Sexual inversion* is another term for homosexuality.) Ellis noted that at first he considered homosexuality "an unpleasant subject," but he found many of those he interviewed to be "persons for whom I felt respect and admiration." He realized that "law and public opinion combine to place a heavy penal (legal) burden and a severe social stigma" on those who are not heterosexual. He wanted to write about gay people as a way of helping heterosexuals understand and accept them.

Ellis's book was ahead of its time in many ways. For instance, he pointed out that while heterosexuals generally considered sex between a man and a woman to be private, they regarded homosexual sex as a public matter. "Whenever a man is openly detected in a homosexual act," Ellis wrote, "however exemplary [admirable] his life may previously have been," heterosexuals felt it "a moral duty to regard the offender as hopelessly damned and to help in hounding him out of society."

Ellis's work, as well as other studies of homosexuality, had positive as well as negative effects. On the plus side, gays and lesbians became aware that many others shared their feelings. Also, sympathetic portrayals of gay people, such as Ellis's, called for understanding of the social problems they faced. On the negative side, the writings drew attention and very often disapproval to gay people as a group.

■ HENRY GERBER AND THE SOCIETY FOR HUMAN RIGHTS

In 1914 World War I (1914–1918) broke out in Europe. The United States joined the fight in 1917 by declaring war on Germany. More than one million Americans served in the military during and after the war. Young Americans who served in Europe gained a broader view of the world. One such American was Henry Gerber.

Gerber had been born in Bavaria (part of modern Germany) before emigrating to Chicago, Illinois, as a young man. He served in the U.S. military from 1920 to 1923 and was stationed in Germany, where the United States kept troops to maintain peace after the war. Gerber was a gay man, and serving in Germany was eye-opening to him. Some German cities at the time had a flourishing gay subculture and gay rights organizations. In his off-hours, Gerber volunteered with such organizations. The United States, he decided, needed a similar organization.

When Gerber returned to Chicago in 1924, he and some friends founded the Society for Human Rights to advocate for gay rights. Using his own typewriter, Gerber began publishing a newsletter, *Friendship and Freedom*.

But the United States of the 1920s was not as progressive about sex as Germany was at the time. At two o'clock on a July night in 1925, police raided Gerber's room in a boardinghouse. Officers seized Gerber's typewriter, his personal diaries, and everything connected to *Friendship and Freedom* and threw Gerber in jail for three days.

One newspaper reported the story of Gerber's arrest with the headline, "Strange Sex Cult Exposed." In court a detective brought forth a powder puff, a fluffy pad with which women apply face powder. The detective claimed to have found the puff in Gerber's room. The puff (which Gerber insisted was not his) was supposed to be evidence of his sexual deviancy—or departure from normal sexual behavior. The court eventually dismissed the case, but in fighting it, Gerber spent all his money. His employer, the U.S. Post Office, fired him for being gay.

> **"Straight [heterosexual] historians are usually terrible judges of anything gay. That's why we are never included in history."**
> —Larry Kramer, *gay rights activist*, 2009

■ ■ ■ NEW YORK CITY IN THE TWENTIES

In the twenties, New York City had one of the country's largest gay and lesbian populations. The city boasted about twenty gay and lesbian bars. In New York's Harlem neighborhood, the annual Hamilton Lodge Ball drew thousands of gay men and lesbians in drag—that is, men dressed as women and women dressed as men. Gay bathhouses, or spas, catered to men of all classes. What's more, gay and lesbian culture was reaching the larger population. For instance, on Broadway, the center of New York's theater district, a play with a lesbian theme, *The God of Vengeance*, played to packed houses in 1922 and 1923.

But gay culture had a formidable foe: the New York Society for the Suppression of Vice. The society did everything in its considerable power to cleanse New York of anything it considered immoral. It targeted books, plays, performances, and any publication that it deemed to be "moral poison." Nude photographs, pamphlets about birth control—the society would have none of it. Anything relating to homosexuality fell squarely within the society's crosshairs.

In 1923 the society filed a complaint against the producer and cast of *The God of Vengeance* for violating obscenity laws. The police arrested the producer and twelve cast members, and a jury found them guilty of giving an immoral performance. The judge released the defendants

Theatergoers could see some gay-themed shows on Broadway (shown in 1925) in the 1920s. But the authorities soon shut the shows down.

without punishment but warned that if they repeated the crime, they would go to prison.

Three years later, a lesbian theme returned to the stage when *The Captive* by Edouard Bourdet opened at Broadway's Empire Theatre. One critic hailed the play as "an expert dramatic production," though he did acknowledge its "revolting theme." Once again, the vice watchdogs launched an attack. The play spurred the New York State Legislature to enact a "padlock bill." Under this law, the authorities could lock the doors of any theater if the owner was convicted of staging an obscene play. In the face of so much legal turmoil, the producers of *The Captive* closed the show voluntarily.

Few authors of this era dared to write books with gay or lesbian themes. Authors sometimes circulated their works in private, among trusted friends. But governments were known to ban published works concerning homosexuality. In 1928 in Britain, for instance, a lesbian writer named Radclyffe Hall published a book called *The Well of Loneliness*. It told the story of a young British woman who had been named Stephen by a father who had hoped for a son. Stephen realizes early in life that she is a lesbian. While serving in the British ambulance corps in World War I, she falls in love with another woman. But their love is doomed by a society that considers lesbian love unnatural and wrong. Stephen herself encourages the woman she loves to leave her for a man, to spare the woman the grief of living in a lesbian-hating society.

The British authorities promptly banned the book after its publication in Britain. Railed James Douglas, editor of the *Sunday Express*, "I would rather give a healthy boy or a healthy girl a [vial] of prussic acid [a deadly poison] than this novel." When a U.S. publisher tried to distribute the book in the United States,

British writer Radclyffe Hall published a book in 1928 about a lesbian relationship. *The Well of Loneliness* was banned in Britain and needed a court order to be sold in the United States.

the New York Society for the Suppression of Vice went to work. It seized 865 copies of the novel from the publisher's New York City office. In court a judge ruled that the book was obscene. On appeal, however, a higher court found the book did not violate obscenity laws. By October 1929, *The Well of Loneliness* had sold eighty thousand copies in the United States.

Radclyffe Hall was born Marguerite Radclyffe Hall in Britain in 1880. Hall, who preferred to go by the name John, lived openly as a lesbian. She wore men's clothing and a very short haircut. She wrote more than a dozen novels and books of poetry but is best known for *The Well of Loneliness*, her only book with an explicitly lesbian theme.

When *The Well of Loneliness* was published in Britain in 1928, British officials (all male) challenged the book in an obscenity trial. One medical official warned that the book would encourage lesbianism and create a "social and national disaster." The British attorney general called the novel "repulsive." The court found the book to be more "corrosive and corruptive than anything ever written," even though the chairman of the court would not allow witnesses in the case to even read it. The British government banned the book in 1928. It was not freely available in Britain again until 1949, when a court overturned the ban.

Hall wrote, "I do not regret having written the book. All that has happened has only served to show me how badly my book was needed. I am proud to have written *The Well of Loneliness*, and I would not alter so much as a comma."

■ YOUNG BAYARD RUSTIN

Bayard Rustin, born in 1912 in West Chester, Pennsylvania, learned early not to make fun of people who were different. When he and some friends called a Chinese man a nasty name, his grandmother made him work in the man's laundry business for two weeks. The Rustins were African American, and Bayard's grandmother was deeply involved with the National Association for the Advancement of Colored People (NAACP). The family was also Quaker, which meant they opposed war. What's more, Bayard was a homosexual.

In high school, Bayard excelled in football and track. He was an excellent singer and an academic standout who won awards for writing and speaking. "He would tackle you, and then get up and recite a poem," said a friend. He also stood up for what he believed in. At the time, racial segregation, or the legal separation of blacks and whites, was common in many parts of the United States. In West Chester, the movie theater had a separate seating area for black moviegoers. Rustin thought that was wrong. He ignored the rule and sat in the main section, reserved for whites.

In 1937 Rustin moved to New York City, where he attended the City College of New York. He lived with his aunt Bessie in Harlem, an African American neighborhood. "Harlem was a totally different world than I had known," Rustin remembered. "In the black upper class there were a great number of gay people. So long as they did not publicize their gayness, there was little or no discussion of it." Gay blacks mingled with straight (heterosexual) ones at Harlem nightclubs and bars.

Rustin remained committed to the fight for social justice and racial equality. He began to work for the Fellowship of Reconciliation (FOR), an interfaith peace and justice organization. He also befriended A. Philip Randolph, the head of the Brotherhood of Sleeping Car Porters, the first black-led U.S. labor union. Right from the beginning, FOR and Randolph recognized Rustin as a superior strategist and a charismatic, persuasive speaker. Rustin clearly was made for big things. With so much going for him, how could anything get in the way of his success?

MORE OF THE SAME

By the 1930s, people had written a smattering of books and plays about homosexuality and published a handful of sympathetic studies. But the attitudes that oppressed gay people had not changed. Homosexuality was still a crime in every state, and no laws protected gay people from discrimination in housing, education, or employment. Most heterosexuals still viewed homosexuality as a perversion.

CHAPTER 2

NEVER FORGET

WORLD WAR II AND THE FORTIES

> Never forget . . . that our bunch
> is going to get someplace if it
> kills us! . . . Agreed? Love, love,
> love, and here's to us all."
>
> —Howard Taylor, World War II serviceman, n.d.

Pat Bond remembers that as a teenager in Davenport, Iowa, around 1940, she felt lonely much of the time. In her diary, she wrote, "I don't know what's wrong with me. Women just don't go around falling in love with women. I guess I'm crazy."

By high school, she realized she was a lesbian. But she found nothing and no one in Davenport to guide her. "You were divorced from parents, from family, from everything," she said. "You were just kind of out there. I looked for some place that I belonged. Always."

Bond's sense of being an outsider was common among gays and lesbians at the time. But serving in the military during World War II (1939–1945) helped some of them realize they were part of a large community.

Approximately sixteen million Americans, male and female, served in the military during World War II. Bond joined the Women's Army Corps, or WAC (its members were called WACs). Like all enlistees, she had to go through a series of examinations, including a mental health exam. The military listed a number of disorders that made a person unfit for military service. One of them was homosexuality.

When Bond arrived at the induction station, an army psychiatrist asked her if she had ever been in love

Women's Army Corps (WAC) members train at a fort in Arizona in 1942. The WAC and other military units banned gay people from serving.

with a woman. Bond lied and became a WAC. Robert Fleischer of New York City did not have to lie. The army psychiatrist asked him, "Do you like girls?" Sure, he liked girls! Not as much as boys, but that's not what the psychiatrist had asked. Fleischer truthfully answered yes, and the army swore in another gay man. Since most gay men and lesbians were well practiced in hiding their true selves from family, friends, and coworkers, concealing the truth from military psychiatrists was not difficult.

■ ■ ■ ■ A NEW COMMUNITY

Wartime service brought millions of men and women into the huge, diverse community of the military, and gay men and lesbians began to find others like themselves. They learned that they were not as alone as they had once believed. On base, in their units, and in the big cities they visited while on leave, they met other gay people.

From the day that Pat Bond arrived for training at Fort Oglethorpe, Georgia, she found other lesbians. Burt Miller, a naval officer from

U.S. soldiers land on the beaches of Normandy, France, on June 6, 1944, to begin the invasion of Europe. Gay soldiers fought and died alongside straight soldiers during World War II. But most gay soldiers kept their sexuality a secret.

Seattle, Washington, was stationed near Los Angeles, California. Walking into the bar of the Biltmore Hotel one evening, he realized the place was packed with fellow gay men. "I was in that bar every night," he recalled. He learned the language of homosexual life, including the term *gay*, which became widely accepted during the war.

> **"Among the bodies lying dead on the battlefields and floating in ocean waters during the war were those of gay American soldiers who had been killed in combat."**
>
> —*Allan Bérubé*, Coming Out Under Fire, 1991

TOLERANCE AND TERROR

At the beginning of World War II, the military treated homosexual sex as a crime. The army imprisoned offenders for up to five years, the navy for up to ten years, before releasing them from service with dishonorable discharges. (A dishonorable discharge is a mark of dishonor. A veteran with a dishonorable discharge receives no military benefits.) At one federal penitentiary (prison), gay prisoners had to wear a big yellow D on their backs. D stood for *degenerate*.

Early in the war, however, military leaders realized they needed to revamp their policies. By following the old policy of imprisoning homosexuals, they surely would run short on prison space and waste valuable time on court cases. Some leaders saw the policy as archaic, or badly outdated. They felt homosexuality should be treated as a psychiatric issue instead of a criminal one.

Thus the military enacted a new policy. It decided to treat homosexuality not as a crime but as a medical problem. Instead of sending them to prison, the military discharged offenders, but only after a review process, usually with confinement first in a locked psychiatric ward, hospital ward, or barracks. Under the old policy, a man or a woman had to be caught in the act of having homosexual sex to be discharged. The new policy was more far-reaching: a person could be discharged just for *being* gay or even for having homosexual tendencies. The policy was all the more unjust in that it relied heavily on suspicions and hearsay rather than facts.

In the face of wartime demands, some officers chose to overlook the new policy, particularly in combat areas. "Lay off my district because you're taking some of my best people away!" ordered one navy admiral. Even General Douglas MacArthur, commander of U.S. forces in the Pacific, is believed to have said, "No more discharges for homosexuals because . . . we have to win the war!" "I found there was a tolerance for lesbianism if they [the military] needed you," said Johnnie Phelps, a WAC. If someone "was needed, they tolerated anything, just about."

But other gay men and lesbians were not so lucky. "They just whisked me away!" remembered Bill Thompson, who served in the navy as a radio operator. One night an armed officer and a marine guard appeared at his door and ordered him to come with them for questioning. "It was like the SS [German secret police] coming in the middle of the night," he says. Other gay sailors and soldiers were taken away in chains.

What came next for many gay men and lesbians was even worse. They found themselves locked up in stockades under armed guard, questioned, humiliated, and abused. Thompson, who was imprisoned at a military base on the island of New Caledonia in the Pacific, remembers that the guards at the stockades treated the gay prisoners like garbage. Guards threatened to make the gay men eat out of trash cans and called them cruel names.

"There was a [guard] called Big John," remembered David Barrett. "He lined us up in front of all the inmates there who were murderers, rapists, thieves—everything you could think of. . . . He told all the rest of them that he thought more of them because we were the scum of the . . . earth."

The men imprisoned on New Caledonia had to march to and from their unit to the mess hall in front of the other soldiers stationed there. "The rest of the hillside was lined with thousands of guys waiting to go

A commanding officer talks to U.S. troops on the Pacific island of New Caledonia during World War II. Gay servicemen at the island's U.S. military base endured harsh imprisonment.

to chow [eat], and the minute we'd start down, there'd be whistles all over the place," said Barrett. The straight men shouted derogatory names for gay men: queers, fruits, faggots, and fairies. "It was just humiliating to go through that three times a day," said Thompson. Another prisoner likened the experience to facing a firing squad. Guards even hung signs over the gay men's holding units. "Queer Stockade," the signs said, or "Queer Brig."

Along with imprisonment came interrogation, or harsh questioning. Interrogators grilled men and women about their sexual encounters, asking about the most intimate details. They tried to get prisoners to name other gay people and used a variety of tactics to get them to talk. Interrogators threatened gay soldiers with criminal prosecution, threatened to tell their families they were gay, and systematically attacked their dignity.

Some gay servicemen and servicewomen outlasted their questioners. They refused to name names or even disclose their sexuality. Others broke down under duress, signed confessions, and identified other gays and lesbians.

The treatment of gays and lesbians in World War II had far-reaching effects. For one, the wartime policy on homosexuals, with its basis in psychiatry, furthered the notion that being gay was a sickness. At the same time, the persecution that gay men and women faced during the war helped them realize that they were part of a larger group and could perhaps challenge this persecution together.

Howard Taylor, locked up in a military hospital, wrote to a gay friend: "Never forget . . . that our bunch is going to get someplace if it kills us! . . . Agreed? Love, love, love, and here's to us all."

RUSTIN: THE WAR YEARS

Bayard Rustin did not serve in World War II. As a Quaker and thus a pacifist (someone who opposes all war), he refused to serve. He could have applied for conscientious objector (CO) status, which would have allowed him to legally avoid military service. But through FOR, he had counseled COs at church-run CO camps. He was incensed to learn that camps in the South were racially segregated, and he refused to willingly participate in segregation. So instead of becoming a CO, he worked as youth secretary for FOR in New York City. He traveled the country for FOR, using his electrifying speaking skills to advocate for peace. In nine months in 1942, he visited twenty states and traveled 10,000 miles (16,000 kilometers).

In his travels, he never shied away from a chance to break down racial barriers. Once, at a midwestern diner, a waitress refused to serve him because he was black. Rustin convinced her and the manager to serve him at the counter, close to the door, to see if the sight of an African American customer would hurt their business as they feared. As it turned out, nobody cared. The manager gave Rustin a free hot meal and from then on served blacks at his diner.

In 1942 Rustin helped found the Congress of Racial Equality

(CORE) to fight for equal rights for African Americans. CORE sought to end discrimination through nonviolent protest, a tactic learned from Indian independence leader Mohandas Gandhi. Rustin worked tirelessly for both FOR and CORE. A. J. Muste, the head of FOR, was thrilled with Rustin's work but not with his sexuality. Muste feared that Rustin's sexual orientation would bring negative attention to both FOR and CORE.

In 1943 the issue of Rustin's sexual orientation became temporarily moot. That year he was arrested for refusing to serve in the military. He spent the next two years in federal prison. When he was released in 1946, he went back to work for FOR and CORE. Once again, his abilities as a magnetic speaker and brilliant strategist propelled him to the forefront of the movement for peace and social justice.

AFTER THE WAR

When the war ended, many gay and lesbian veterans settled in big cities such as New York, Chicago, and San Francisco. Their wartime experiences had shown them that big cities, unlike small towns, offered at least some semblance of a gay community. Even heartland cities such as Kansas City and Cleveland had gay bars.

Pat Bond chose to stay in the WAC after the war. But in the postwar years, the army, navy, and other military branches stepped up their purges of gays and lesbians. Bond described it as a witch hunt—the searching out of minorities or those with unpopular views for harassment and persecution. She recalls that the army "started an incredible witch hunt" in Tokyo, Japan, where she was stationed. "Every day there were court-martials and trials. You were there testifying against your friends, or they were testifying against you."

Bond continued, "They called up one of our kids—Helen. They got her up on the stand and told her that if she didn't give the names of her friends they would tell her parents she was gay. She went up to her room on the sixth floor and jumped out and killed herself. She was twenty."

Johnnie Phelps, a lesbian and a WAC, served on General Dwight D. Eisenhower's staff in Europe after World War II. Eisenhower had heard that lesbians were serving in his WAC battalion. He asked Phelps to make up a list of names.

Phelps said yes, she would make him that list. But she reminded him that the battalion was highly decorated (that is, its members had won a lot of medals), had a notably low number of pregnancies and absentees, and had a superb record.

"I'll make your list," Phelps told the general, "but you've got to know that when you get the list back, my name's going to be first."

Overhearing her, Eisenhower's female secretary added, "Sir, if the General pleases, Sergeant Phelps will have to be second on the list. My name will be first."

Eisenhower looked at them, shook his head, and said, "Forget that order."

■ THE KINSEY REPORT

In 1948 an 804-page, 3-pound (1.4-kilogram) book hit the best-seller lists. *Sexual Behavior in the Human Male*, by scientist Alfred C. Kinsey, presented the results of Kinsey's extensive study of male sexuality. Kinsey's research indicated that 85 percent of American males engaged

American author and scientist Alfred C. Kinsey wrote a book about male sexual behavior in 1948. His research revealed that many men had homosexual experiences.

in premarital sex and that at least one-third of married men had extramarital affairs. One of Kinsey's most noteworthy findings, though, was that 37 percent of males between adolescence and old age had had some kind of sexual experience with another male. This number was far higher than anyone expected. Kinsey also noted that 10 percent of men between the ages of sixteen and fifty-five had been almost exclusively homosexual for at least three years.

Kinsey's book was the talk of the nation. The Kinsey Report, as the book became known, sold two hundred thousand copies in less than two months. "Not since *Gone With the Wind* had booksellers seen anything like it," noted *Time* magazine in March 1948, referring to the massive best seller of 1936.

In the postwar years, Gore Vidal (*below*) was considered one of the most promising writers in the United States. By his early twenties, he had published two books, both of which were highly praised by critics. Then his third book appeared. In *The City and the Pillar*, Vidal wrote forthrightly about a sexual relationship between two masculine and athletic men. "I knew that my description of the love affair between two 'normal' all-American boys . . . would challenge every superstition about sex in my native land," said Vidal. "Until then, American novels of 'inversion' [homosexuality] dealt with transvestites or with lonely bookish boys who married unhappily and pined for Marines. I broke that mold."

The City and the Pillar sparked outrage on nearly every front. The *New York Times* refused to accept advertisements for it. The *Washington Post* book reviewer was revolted by its "slimy subject." It took years for Vidal's career to recover. Yet *The City and the Pillar* has never gone out of print. It ranks number 17 on the roster of 100 Best Lesbian and Gay Novels, a list issued by the Publishing Triangle, an association of gays and lesbians in publishing.

On the face of things, it seemed that the Kinsey Report would help public understanding of homosexuality. After all, if so many people had homosexual experiences, perhaps homosexuality was normal? As noted in the *New York Times*, the report "presents facts that indicate the necessity to review some of our legal and moral concepts." And what about the psychiatric community? Could psychiatrists really label so many people "sick" for what was clearly widespread behavior?

As it turned out, the report had both good and bad effects. On the positive side, the Kinsey Report assured gay men that they were not deviant, or abnormal but were part of a very large community. On the other hand, for those who saw homosexuality as evil or sick, the Kinsey Report was evidence of a national scourge, one that had to be dealt with by any means necessary.

CHAPTER 3

THE
FEAR
THE FIFTIES

"If you could only
understand the fear."

—Del Martin, cofounder of Daughters of Bilitis, discussing
the antigay climate of the 1950s, 1976

By 1950 the United States was in the middle of the Cold War (1945–1991) with the Soviet Union (fifteen republics that included Russia). This conflict was marked by mistrust and hostility between the two superpowers, but they did not fight each other directly. The Soviet Union was a Communist country. Under the Soviet form of Communism, the central government controlled all business and economic activity. It denied people basic freedoms, such as the right to vote, freedom of speech, and freedom of religion. People in the Soviet Union could not choose where to live or where to work. The government controlled everything in their lives. The authorities imprisoned and frequently executed people who challenged the system.

In the 1930s and 1940s, some Americans had been drawn to Communism, which in theory promised to distribute society's wealth equally among everyone. But by the 1950s, many Americans feared Communism. They saw how the Soviet government abused its citizens. They distrusted anyone with ties to Communism, such as those who joined the U.S. Communist Party.

The public feared that Communist spies were active in the United States, and some U.S. politicians—most notably Senator Joseph McCarthy of Wisconsin—pumped up this fear. In February

U.S. senator Joseph McCarthy of Wisconsin talks at a Senate subcommittee in March 1950. McCarthy's hunt for Communists in the federal government paved the way for an equally ruthless purge of homosexuals from government jobs.

1950, McCarthy made a speech in Wheeling, West Virginia. "I have here in my hand a list of 205" people employed by the State Department, he announced, "that were known to the Secretary of State as being members of the Communist Party." McCarthy said the federal government needed to rid itself of anyone who supported Communism.

Later in February, Styles Bridges, a Republican senator from New Hampshire, questioned Secretary of State Dean Acheson and his deputy, John Peurifoy, in a Senate subcommittee hearing. Bridges was eager to portray the Democratic administration of President Harry Truman as soft on Communism. He wanted to know whether Acheson and his staff were aggressively rooting out Communists in the federal government. "How many [employees] have resigned under investigation?" Bridges grilled Acheson and Peurifoy.

"Ninety-one persons in the shady category," responded Peurifoy. "Most of those were homosexuals." Aha. Homosexuals. That remark set the ball rolling. Not only were gay people "perverts" in the public imagination, but Peurifoy suggested that they were also subversives, or enemies of the government.

In the weeks following Peurifoy's remark, U.S. senators from both parties argued over "what further action the group should take to meet the security threat posed by perverts on Government payrolls." Thus began a witch hunt for gays in the federal government and beyond. The argument was that gay government employees were not only disloyal but were also security risks, or likely to reveal government secrets. Suppose Communist agents pressured a gay federal employee to pass on secret information. The Communists might threaten blackmail—in this case, to expose his sexuality—if he refused.

Lieutenant Roy Blick, head of the vice squad in Washington, D.C., stoked the fires of suspicion. He estimated that there were five thousand "perverts" in the city and that 75 percent of them were employed by the federal government. This news prompted the hiring of more vice officers and the sharing of information between federal government agencies about gay staff members.

"The names of about 200 sex perverts in Government jobs here—men and women alike—have been turned over to their employing agencies by the Civil Service Commission," reported the *Washington Post* in a front page story. "Many of them either have been or will be fired as unsuited for Government work."

When Dwight D. Eisenhower became president in 1953, things got worse for gay government employees. Eisenhower signed Executive Order 10450, which required the firing of any employee determined to be guilty of "sexual perversion." Each month the government fired between forty and sixty gay people.

Executive Order 10450 also called for the Federal Bureau of Investigation (FBI) to supply information on gays and lesbians to the Civil Service Commission, the agency responsible for hiring federal employees. The FBI worked aggressively with police departments across the country to access a vast number of arrest records. If it found an old arrest record for homosexuality in Des Moines, Iowa, for a gay federal employee, it turned the information over to the employee's supervisor. In fact, the FBI shared such information with private employers as well.

Throughout this period, few people questioned the assumption that gay people were susceptible to blackmail. Yet Max Lerner, a columnist with the *New York Post*, had conducted extensive research for a twelve-part series, "Washington Sex Story," published in 1950. "At no point was I able to track down a single case" of a homosexual falling prey to blackmail, he wrote.

Eventually McCarthyism—the anti-Communist hysteria—ended when a few brave people began standing up to Senator McCarthy and his supporters. Almost nobody took a similar stand to protest the purge of gays and lesbians.

NATIONWIDE REPRESSION

Antigay attitudes were hardly limited to the federal government. In the 1950s, most white, middle-class Americans held confining social and sexual views. Television shows of the era depicted the "ideal" family: a working father who always knew best; a happy, stay-at-home wife who dressed up to clean the house; and a couple of squeaky-clean kids. Everybody was unquestionably straight—and almost always white.

Many Americans of this era feared and loathed anything that challenged social norms. They bought into widespread myths about homosexuality, including the myth that gay people recruited straight people—especially children—into their ranks. Much of the public imagined gay men and lesbians as shady characters who prowled the streets for straight victims and "infected" them with homosexuality. Since few gay people dared to be open about their sexuality, straight Americans didn't realize how far this image was from the truth. They didn't know that some of their own friends, neighbors, and coworkers were gay.

The law reflected the public's fears. In big cities, the police freely raided gay bars, which were practically the only public places gay men and women could socialize in at the time. In 1955 police in Baltimore, Maryland, arrested 162 men during a raid on the Pepper Hill Club. In 1956 police in San Francisco raided the Alamo Club, a lesbian bar, and sent thirty-six women to jail.

The repression wasn't just directed at sexual minorities. It targeted any person or group that threatened social or political norms. In Florida a state legislative committee called the Johns Committee, led by one-time governor Charley Johns, hunted the halls of public schools and colleges. Committee members looked for "subversives," which they defined as homosexuals, Communists, and activists for African American civil rights. The committee's efforts resulted in hundreds of university professors, students, and public school teachers and administrators being fired or suspended.

In Greensboro, North Carolina, police relied on informants to try thirty-two men for having gay sex. For "crimes against nature," twenty-four of the men went to prison for terms of five to twenty years. When someone kidnapped, sexually assaulted, and murdered two children in Sioux City, Iowa, the city reacted by rounding up twenty gay men and committing them to a mental hospital. None of the men had anything to do with the crimes.

In 1952 the American Psychiatric Association (APA) published its first edition of *The Diagnostic and Statistical Manual of Mental Disorders*. Homosexuality, said the manual, was a sociopathic personality disturbance. In other words, gay people were mentally ill. What's more, most psychiatrists thought that homosexuality was treatable and could be cured.

Many gay people greeted this news with relief. The APA said they weren't criminals. They were simply suffering from a mental disorder. And if they were sick, shouldn't they be treated with compassion, not punishment?

Evelyn Hooker, a psychology professor at the University of California, Los Angeles, disagreed with the APA. Persuaded by a gay friend to conduct a scientific study, she administered psychological tests to thirty gay men and thirty straight men. Her results, published in the mid-1950s, showed that gay men were at least as well adjusted as straight ones. At the time, though, the psychiatric community was too convinced of its own diagnosis to listen to Hooker.

One important voice was missing in the discussion: the gay person's. In 1951 Donald Webster Cory, a gay man writing under a pseudonym (pen name), published *The Homosexual in America*. Homosexuality was not a sickness, Cory wrote. He said that people were born gay, not "recruited" by older homosexuals. He argued that gays and lesbians constituted a minority that needed to organize and advocate for equal rights and acceptance.

■ ■ ■ ■ "IT WAS LIKE A HORROR MOVIE"

In the early fifties, a mental hospital seemed to many people like the logical place for gays and lesbians. Since World War II, the opinion of the psychiatric community that homosexuality was a sickness had gained wider acceptance. What's more, some psychiatrists maintained that homosexuality could be cured with proper treatment.

When people are told they are sick and wrong often enough, they start to believe the worst of themselves. For instance, some black children who were repeatedly taught they were inferior to whites came to believe it. Similarly, in a hostile environment, some men and women who were attracted to members of their own sex thought they were indeed sick. Many suffered alone, in silence and depression. Others began seeking or were pressured into psychiatric treatment.

Some of the "treatments" for homosexuality were barbaric. In aversion therapy, for instance, psychiatrists showed patients images to awaken their sexual desire. For example, a doctor might show a gay man pictures of attractive naked men. Then the doctor subjected the patient to a painful stimulus, such as electric shocks. From then on, the patient associated same-sex desire with pain—or so the theory went. Some doctors used more drastic measures, such as lobotomies (removal of part of a person's brain) or, for lesbians, hysterectomies (removal of the uterus).

One psychiatrist, Charles Socarides, became known as a national expert on homosexuality. He claimed that a domineering mother and an aloof father caused boys to grow up to be gay. The media turned to him so often that his assertions regarding homosexuality, wrong as they were, became the dominant viewpoint.

Some parents, alarmed to learn their children were gay, sought psychiatric help for them. As a lesbian teenager in the 1950s, "Whitey" was subjected to a range of bizarre treatments. "The psychiatrist put me on two green salads a day," she said. Later, her parents committed her to a state mental hospital, where she stayed for four years. "I was on tranquilizers; they almost killed me with them," she remembered. "It was like a horror movie."

◼ HARRY HAY AND MATTACHINE

Harry Hay, a gay man in Los Angeles, was alarmed at the campaign against same-sex love. He felt that people like him needed to organize to protect themselves. As a young man, he had learned about Henry Gerber and his attempts to organize gay people in Chicago. Hay never forgot Gerber's story.

Hay and a friend gathered a small group of gay men. They suggested that gays take action to challenge their unfair treatment. In response, they got "a terrified silence," writes historian John D'Emilio. Societal repression was so effective that "no one was willing to risk the exposure of his sexual identity by joining a homosexual rights organization."

Harry Hay *(left)* poses for a photo in the early 1960s. Hay started the Mattachine Society in California in 1951. The secret organization worked for equal rights for gay men and lesbians.

Eventually, Hay and his friends started a series of discussion groups for gay men and lesbians. From these meetings, they created a secret organization called the Mattachine Society in 1951. (In the Middle Ages in France, Mattachines were unmarried men who danced in masks at festivals.) The organization met in secret, and only members knew the identities of other members. The group gave members something they had never experienced before: "We had found a sense of belonging," said James Gruber.

One of the practices the Mattachines opposed was police entrapment. In the 1950s, plainclothes police officers would pose as gay men in

A rare photo of the Mattachine Society in Los Angeles, California, including founder Harry Hay *(top left, dark shirt)*. The group worked to defend member Dale Jennings *(far left, white shirt)* after his arrest for "lewd conduct."

popular gay cruising areas—places where men gathered for sexual encounters. A police officer in disguise would proposition a gay man and then arrest him for lewd conduct. Even when the entrapment was illegal, almost no one challenged it, because the victim risked further public exposure if he contested the charge. Then police entrapped and arrested Dale Jennings, a Mattachine member. With Mattachine's support, Jennings fought the charge.

To protect its members' identities, Mattachine created a separate legal chapter, the Citizens Committee to Outlaw Entrapment, to fight on Jennings's behalf. The committee distributed fliers about the case in gay bars, at beaches, and in other places where gay people congregated. The gay community responded with donations toward legal fees.

In the June 1952 trial, Jennings said that, yes, he was gay. But he pleaded innocent to the charges of lewd behavior. Ultimately, the district attorney dropped the charges against Jennings.

After the case, Mattachine grew quickly. Within a year, the number of members, male and female, had increased to two thousand. New chapters formed in other cities. In January 1953, a Mattachine member extended the group's reach by launching ONE: *The Homosexual Magazine*. About two thousand subscribers received the magazine by mail each month. By 1955 New York City had a Mattachine chapter.

But along with the growth in Mattachine membership came disagreement about the organization's goals. The original members maintained that gays and lesbians should fight for equal rights and acceptance as a minority group within the United States. But many new members bristled at the term *minority*. They hated being thought of as different just because of their sexual orientation. They wanted to be accepted into mainstream, heterosexual society, not set apart.

What's more, Harry Hay had once been in the U.S. Communist Party, which appalled many new members. Hay's ties to Communism would cast suspicion on everyone associated with Mattachine, they feared. So Harry Hay bowed out of the organization he had founded. He didn't want his Communist past to interfere with what he hoped Mattachine could accomplish.

ONE GOES TO COURT

In 1954 the U.S. Post Office and the FBI declared the gay publication ONE to be obscene. The Post Office refused to mail the October 1954 issue, which included a short story about a lesbian couple. The group that published the magazine sued in federal court. When it lost in the lower courts, it appealed to the U.S. Supreme Court. The Court accepted the case, the first time it took a case involving gay rights. In a unanimous decision in 1958, the Court ruled in ONE's favor and removed legal barriers to mailing the magazine. The ruling was the first major legal victory for gay rights.

> Mattachine's members knew all too well the pain and bewilderment of growing up gay in a heterosexual society. Thus, at their induction into the society, members swore their support to young gays and lesbians. They vowed "that no boy or girl, approaching the maelstrom [chaos] of [a gay adolescence], need make that crossing alone."

The new Mattachine was very different from the one Hay first envisioned. It was no longer a secret society. In 1959 the society held its annual convention in Denver, Colorado, and members boldly chose visibility over secrecy. Not only did they hold a public press conference, members used their own names and even allowed themselves to be photographed. A few weeks later, Denver police raided the homes of local Mattachine officers. One man was imprisoned, and others lost their jobs.

DAUGHTERS OF BILITIS

Del Martin and Phyllis Lyon, a lesbian couple in San Francisco, did not care for the gay bar scene. Yet they wanted a place where lesbians could socialize. In 1955, along with three other lesbian couples, they created Daughters of Bilitis (DOB). DOB was created as "a very secret lesbian social club," said Martin. Even its name was deliberately obscure. It came from a work by French poet Pierre Louÿs about a lesbian named Bilitis. "If anyone asked us, we could always say we belong to a poetry club," Martin and Lyon later explained.

Phyllis Lyon *(left)* and Del Martin *(right)* created a secret social club for lesbians in the mid-1950s in San Francisco, California. Daughters of Bilitis allowed lesbians to socialize with other lesbians.

The organization held meetings and began publishing a newsletter called *The Ladder*. Like Mattachine, the group's ability to expand its reach was hampered by members' dread of exposure. "If you could only understand the fear," Martin explained. "And we [the leadership] were just as scared as everyone else."

DISCARDING BAYARD

In January 1953, Bayard Rustin had just delivered an inspiring talk about world peace to the American Association of University Women in Pasadena, California. Later that evening, police discovered him in a parked car with two other gay men and arrested them all on a "morals charge."

Convicted, Rustin served sixty days in the Los Angeles County Jail. Worse still was the damage to his career. Throughout his tenure with the Fellowship of Reconciliation, his sexuality had troubled his superiors. Rustin offered to resign, and A. J. Muste accepted his resignation.

Rustin had trouble finding a new job. He worked moving furniture for a short time. One social worker suggested he look for a position as a butler. After several months, he went to work for the War Resisters League, an antiwar group.

Then, on December 1, 1955, in Montgomery, Alabama, civil rights activist Rosa Parks refused to give up her seat to a white man on a crowded city bus, as required by law. A police officer arrested her. The event galvanized Montgomery's black community. In no time, they had organized a boycott—refusing to use the city bus system that discriminated against them.

A. Philip Randolph knew there was no better strategist and organizer in the United States than Bayard Rustin. At Randolph's suggestion, Rustin went to Montgomery to help with the boycott. He began advising Dr. Martin Luther King Jr., the young pastor who was leading the movement, on how to use nonviolent protest to achieve change. Rustin soon became one of King's most valuable advisers. He was instrumental in developing the Southern Christian Leadership Conference (SCLC), which King led, to challenge segregation.

But when King and other members of the SCLC learned about Rustin's sexual orientation and his arrest, they worried. What if word got out about his background? The information could hurt King and damage the civil rights movement. Adam Clayton Powell, a black U.S. congressman from New York, was particularly outspoken about Rustin. In 1960 he threatened to release a false story that Rustin and King were having a sexual relationship if King didn't dismiss Rustin. While King took his time deciding what to do, Rustin decided it was best to simply resign. He returned to the War Resisters League.

FRANK KAMENY: NOT MOST PEOPLE

By the time Frank Kameny was six years old, he knew he wanted to be an astronomer. He graduated from high school at the age of sixteen, served combat duty in Europe during World War II, and studied astronomy at Harvard University on a scholarship. In 1957 he was working for the Army Map Service in Washington, D.C. His future looked promising. Space exploration was just beginning, and Harvard-trained astronomers would be in great demand.

One day federal investigators contacted Kameny. "Information has come to the attention of the U.S. Civil Service Commission that you are a homosexual," the investigators said. "What comment, if any, do you care to make?"

Kameny *was* a homosexual. Most people in his shoes would have quietly packed their things and resigned, but Frank Kameny was not most people. He informed the investigators that his private life was none of the federal government's business. The government fired him.

Kameny knew the government was wrong and began to fight his dismissal. He filed an unsuccessful appeal through the government's internal appeal process and then took his case to the courts. The case went all the way to the U.S. Supreme Court, which dismissed it.

Meanwhile, Kameny could not land a job. As the months passed, he ran out of money. He turned to the Salvation Army for food. "For about eight months in 1959 I was living on twenty cents' worth of food a day, which, even by 1959 prices, was not much. A big day was when I could afford twenty-five cents and put a pat of margarine on my frankfurters and potatoes," he remembered.

Finally, after twenty months, he found a job. But his fight for gay rights had only just begun.

NEW YORK CITY

Through the 1950s, New York City continued to draw gays and lesbians. They came not because the city welcomed them. In fact, New York City was infamous for its regular crackdowns on gay men especially. Police raided gay bars and arrested scores of gay men through entrapment. But the city was huge—big enough for a gay person to find both a community and anonymity—the state of being unknown and private. Plus, New York was hopping. It had scads of gay bars. To discourage gay bars, the New York State Liquor Authority made it difficult for bar owners to serve drinks to gays and lesbians. So the Mafia, which skirted the law and paid off the police, got in the business of running gay bars.

The city's dynamic arts scene was a draw as well. Gay and

Author James Baldwin wrote about the pressures of being gay and African American as early as the 1950s.

lesbian writers, painters, actors, designers, and dancers flocked to New York. In the 1950s, Arthur Laurents, Leonard Bernstein, Stephen Sondheim, and Jerome Robbins—all gay or bisexual— were busy creating the Broadway show *West Side Story*. Choreographer Merce Cunningham and avant-garde composer John Cage were collaborating on new modern dance works. Gay, African American writer James Baldwin was hosting fellow writers at his studio apartment on Horatio Street. A few blocks away, on Perry Street, May Swenson was writing poetry in the apartment she shared with her female partner.

Baldwin and Swenson lived in Greenwich Village, which had a long history as an artists' haven. The rest of the country might be idolizing Ozzie and Harriet, the perfect TV parents, but in Greenwich Village, a nonconformist could feel at home. Thus Greenwich Village had a sizable gay and lesbian population.

One chunk of the city's gay population had no home whatsoever. These were young gay runaways, many of whom had come to New York City after their families had kicked them out. They often gravitated to Times Square, where they relied on hustling (male prostitution) to survive.

Through it all, gay and lesbian life in New York City "was furtive [secretive]," remembered Jack Dowling. "Furtive is a good way to describe the fifties." It would be a less apt description of the sixties.

In 1952 George Jorgensen, a twenty-six-year-old former soldier, traveled from New York to Denmark. There he endured a series of operations and approximately twenty thousand hormone shots. Soon afterward, Jorgensen sent a letter to his parents: "My dears, nature made a mistake, which I have corrected, and I am now your daughter." Jorgensen signed the letter Christine instead of George. The surgery and hormone shots had turned the former man into an attractive woman.

The press came out in full force to cover Christine's return home (*below front*). Her father, awaiting her arrival, wasn't sure how to refer to his offspring. Him? Her? He settled on calling her "the youngster."

Jorgensen became a media star. Her classy manner made her an excellent ambassador for transsexuals—biological males who feel like women inside and biological females who feel like men inside. Jorgensen raised Americans' awareness of transsexuals and inspired others to undergo sex reassignment surgery.

CHAPTER 4

SO BOLD
THE SIXTIES

"So here is a story of bravery,
in a time when it was rare for
gay people to be so bold."

—Frank Fitch, member of the Society for Individual Rights, 1973

In 1960 the United States elected a new, young president, John F. Kennedy. He had fresh ideas and lofty ideals. A dynamic era of cutting-edge technology and space exploration had begun. Civil rights activists taking courageous actions were stirring hope that racial justice would become a reality.

For gays and lesbians, though, things were as bad as ever. When the decade began, the laws regarding homosexuality in the United States were more severe than those in Cuba and the Soviet Union, nations known for their oppressive governments. Two men found having sex, even in the privacy of their own home, could be punished with anything from a fine to a life sentence. Gay people could, by law, be subjected to such punishments as electroshock therapy or lobotomies. In New York, police could arrest a person who was wearing fewer than three articles of clothing specific to his or her sex. Officers used the law to nab transvestites.

NEW YORK CITY: YOUNG ACTIVISTS

Craig Rodwell, who grew up in Chicago, realized he was gay as a teenager. He heard about the Mattachine Society a few years later. When Rodwell learned that New York City was home to a large branch of Mattachine and a huge gay population, he made up his mind to move there. He saved money by working different jobs, and at the age of eighteen, in the summer of 1958, he arrived in Manhattan.

Rodwell had expected New York City's largest gay organization to be full of activists. But at a Mattachine discussion group, he found most of the members to be older and conservative. Their focus was not activism but education. They invited speakers to address the group. The typical speaker was a straight, psychiatric "expert" who spent the evening explaining their sexuality to them. The whole business made Rodwell impatient.

He turned his energies to volunteering in the small Mattachine office and virtually took over the society's newsletter. At first he used a pseudonym on the masthead—the section of the paper that listed staff members' names—as the other members did. As always, staffers worried they'd be fired or evicted if they openly declared their sexuality. But hiding wasn't Rodwell's style. Before long, he was using his own name.

Rodwell's life was not solely about politics. For a time, he dated a man ten years his senior named Harvey Milk. Milk romanced him with flowers and meals but stopped short of joining Rodwell in his activist pursuits. Milk had a prestigious job in the insurance business. He was not interested in the gay rights movement—not then at least.

Randy Wicker, another young gay man in New York, also found the Mattachine Society overly cautious. Like Rodwell, he yearned to take an activist approach. His outspokenness made the more conservative Mattachine members nervous. "He was, let's say, a disturbing acquisition to the movement," remembered a former Mattachine Society president.

Wicker broke away from Mattachine and in 1962 formed his own organization, a group he liked to call the Powerful Homosexual League of New York. It had all of one member: himself. He printed business cards and went to work to change the public's view of homosexuals. One thing that really angered Wicker was when heterosexual "experts," such as psychiatrists, spoke to the media about what gay people were like. If straight people wanted to know what a gay person was like, shouldn't they ask a gay person?

Wicker arranged for a group of eight gay men to talk about their lives on a ninety-minute radio broadcast for New York station WBAI.

A bartender refuses to serve Mattachine Society members John Timmins, Dick Leitsch, Craig Rodwell, and Randy Wicker at a New York City bar in 1966. The men were challenging a law that made it illegal to serve alcohol to gay customers by staging a protest they called a "sip-in."

WBAI and Wicker both publicized the broadcast, and the New York Times, Newsweek, and other publications reported on the groundbreaking program. The show and the publicity it received helped create at least some understanding of gay men and their problems.

■ MATTACHINE SOCIETY OF WASHINGTON, D.C.

In Washington, D.C., Frank Kameny realized that he could work for change more effectively as part of an organization than as an individual. In November 1961, he founded the Mattachine Society of Washington, D.C. (MSW), with Jack Nichols. Nichols was younger than Kameny and more forthright about his sexuality than most gay men of the era. Not only had he told his high school friends in Bethesda, Maryland, that he was gay, but he had also given them each a copy of Donald Webster Cory's book The Homosexual in America.

The MSW was a far cry from the Mattachine chapters that focused on education. MSW was all about political activism and change, and the federal government was its first target. Bruce Scott, a Mattachine member, had been fired from his job at the U.S. Labor Department and refused a job at the Defense Department because of his sexual orientation. Many gay men had stood in his shoes. Scott, however, was willing to publicly acknowledge that he was gay and file a lawsuit, claiming discrimination.

MSW persuaded the local affiliate of the American Civil Liberties Union (ACLU) to take Scott's case. The ACLU works to protect the rights and freedoms of Americans through legal and educational work. The organization filed *Scott v. Macy* in 1963, and in 1965, the federal court of appeals ruled in Bruce Scott's favor. If the government was going to fire someone for being gay, noted the court, it had to establish what sexuality had to do with job performance.

By the time the court decided *Scott v. Macy*, the MSW had racked up other successes. It had set up a referral service for gays in need of lawyers, doctors, and clergymen. It wrote letters to scores of government officials requesting meetings. A few officials did meet with society members, but others were less welcoming. Congressman Paul C. Jones of Missouri responded, "Please do not contaminate my mail with such filthy trash."

BARBARA GITTINGS AND THE DOB

Barbara Gittings knew as an adolescent that she was attracted to other women. When she searched her college library for an explanation of her sexuality, though, she encountered terms like *sexual perversion*. "That's me they're writing about—but it's not like me at all," she thought. She dropped out of college and ended up in New York City, where in 1958 she founded a chapter of Daughters of Bilitis. She appreciated the social outlet that DOB provided, yet she yearned to expand the group into something more meaningful. In 1963 she met Frank Kameny.

"Until I met Frank, I had only a muddled sense of what we could do as activists," she said. "Frank crystallized my thinking." Gittings

Barbara Gittings plans *The Ladder* publication schedule in the mid-1960s. She wanted the publication to be up front about its lesbian focus.

became editor of *The Ladder,* and she made the DOB publication a vehicle for a more activist agenda. For instance, she added a subtitle, *A Lesbian Review.* There would be no more hiding behind an ambiguous name. She put photographs of lesbians on the cover. She wanted to show that lesbians were as happy and normal as any other women.

Gittings's changes were too much for the older members of DOB. They were not ready to exchange anonymity for activism, and they fired Gittings as editor. Being fired did nothing to dissuade Gittings.

BAYARD RUSTIN AND THE MARCH

The civil rights movement seemed to gain momentum every day. African American activists held sit-ins and demonstrations. They held "Freedom Rides" to protest segregation on interstate buses. Through it all, Bayard Rustin was forced to watch from the sidelines.

A. Philip Randolph, the movement's elder statesman, had never stopped believing in Rustin. In July 1963, Randolph called a meeting of civil rights activists, including Rustin. He was planning a huge march on Washington to call for jobs and equal rights for African Americans, and he needed someone to organize the massive effort under a tight timeline. He wanted Rustin.

Roy Wilkins, head of the NAACP, objected. Rustin, he said, "had too many scars." Wilkins thought that Rustin's sexuality and his Pasadena arrest record would jeopardize the march. Randolph finally gave in and then announced that he would direct the march himself. But that meant he could choose his own deputy, and "I want Bayard to be my deputy," he said.

So for the next month and a half, Rustin worked tirelessly to organize the March on Washington for Jobs and Freedom, scheduled for August 28, 1963. "This was Bayard at his best," remembers civil rights leader John Lewis. He "directed dozens of volunteers who were

Many civil rights leaders condemned Bayard Rustin *(left)* for being gay. A. Philip Randolph (talking into microphone) was an exception.

working around the clock" and coordinated "an army of organizers in virtually every major city in the nation." He didn't miss a detail, right down to making sure the event had enough toilets, blankets, and buses.

Just days before the march, a newspaper article revealed Rustin's arrest record as part of an otherwise favorable profile. Senator Strom Thurmond of South Carolina seized on the information and attacked Rustin from the Senate floor. He aimed to use Rustin's sexuality to discredit the march and the civil rights movement.

Despite the attack, the march went ahead as planned. On August 28, the March on Washington for Jobs and Freedom drew a quarter of a million people. They arrived on two thousand buses and twenty-one chartered trains. The marchers included sixty thousand white people, including Frank Kameny. The high point of the day came when Martin Luther King delivered his rousing "I have a dream" speech—calling for a world of racial equality—at the Lincoln Memorial.

Rustin considered it "one of the great days in American history," and most historians would agree. That the day came off basically without a hitch and drew such a phenomenal crowd is undoubtedly because of Bayard Rustin. That Rustin rarely gets the credit he deserves for the march is because of his sexuality.

■ PICKETS

One wet Saturday in November 1964, a small group of men and women, mostly gay, gathered in front of the Armed Forces Induction Center on Whitehall Street in New York City. They had come to protest the military ban on gays and lesbians. They picketed, or marched with signs, in front of the building. Never before had gay people picketed for their rights in the United States. Picketing meant taking a public stand, and in 1964, it was dangerous to take that risk.

Randy Wicker, who organized the picket, was willing to risk it. So was Craig Rodwell and Daughters of Bilitis members Nancy Garden and Renee Cafiero. "It was a nasty, rainy day," remembers Garden. "We were very nervous—okay, scared—for we had no idea what to expect." Would passersby taunt them or even try to hurt them?

They took care to look respectable. Garden and Cafiero wore skirts "to look as 'normal' as possible," Garden notes.

Hoisting signs, the picketers marched in a circle in front of the center, ready for whatever trouble might come their way. As it turned out, they had no trouble at all. "Not too many people were outside, given the weather," says Garden, "and Whitehall Street on a weekend wasn't exactly a hotbed of activity anyway."

Afterward, the participants in the nation's first picket for gay rights slipped into a restaurant to warm up. "We felt a little let down because it had been so uneventful," Garden explains, "but also triumphant, since we'd actually done it!"

Soon after, MSW launched a series of pickets around the nation's capital. Ten picketers participated in the first one, on April 17, 1965. They included Frank Kameny and Jack Nichols.

"Kameny had insisted that we seven men must wear suits and ties, and the women, dresses and [high] heels," recalled Nichols. It was of paramount importance to him that gay men and lesbians come across as respectable citizens, not the "deviates" of the straight public's imagination. "A few tourists gawked and there were one or two snickers," said Nichols, but overall the picket went off without incident.

Through 1965 and 1966, MSW picketed the Pentagon (U.S. military headquarters in Washington, D.C.,) to challenge the ban on gays in the military. It also picketed the U.S. State Department and the Civil Service Commission. At the time, picketing was a bold statement of dissent. The group held its last picket in April 1966 in front of the White House. Barbara Gittings was there, and so was Craig Rodwell. Altogether, nearly seventy people participated.

It was "the most wonderful day of my life," Rodwell said—so wonderful that he and the others hated to see it end. Rodwell came up with an idea: Every year on July 4, they would picket Philadelphia's Independence Hall, where the Declaration of Independence had been adopted, to remind Americans that gay people lacked the basic rights of life, liberty, and the pursuit of happiness, which the declaration called for. They would call their picket the Annual Reminder.

The Annual Reminder at Independence Hall in Philadelphia, Pennsylvania, was a chance for gay rights activists to remind people about discrimination against gay Americans. These picketers are shown at the Annual Reminder in 1967.

SAN FRANCISCO: RAIDS AND RIOTS

In 1964 a young minister, Ted McIlvenna, started a new job. He was assigned to the Glide Memorial Methodist Church in San Francisco's Tenderloin district, a tough area known for drug dealing and male and female prostitution. Taking his job into the streets, McIlvenna learned that some of the male prostitutes were just teenagers. Their parents had kicked them out of the house for being gay, and they scraped out a meager living by hustling.

McIlvenna helped the young people with their immediate needs, such as food and shelter, but he wanted to do more. He brought in ministers Don Kuhn and Cecil Williams to help. With more staff, Glide created Vanguard, an organization for gay street youth, which published its own magazine, *V*.

McIlvenna brought together more San Francisco clergymen to form the Council on Religion and the Homosexual (CRH). This organization worked to educate clergy about homosexuality and to advance the cause of gay rights. At the time, most organized religions condemned homosexuality as a sin. Many gays and lesbians, feeling shunned, had given up organized religion altogether. But here was the CRH reaching out to them and working to advance their cause nationwide.

Also in 1964, gay leaders in San Francisco created the Society for Individual Rights (SIR), which sought to serve the needs of a wide cross section of the city's gay population. SIR opened the first gay community center in the United States. It also sponsored dances and classes, opened a thrift shop, and conducted voter registration drives.

But San Francisco's gay citizens faced hostility from much of the city. When CRH decided to hold a costume ball as a fund-raiser on New Year's Day 1965, organizers had trouble finding a venue willing to rent them space.

"One hotel after another turned them down," reported *Town Talk*, a gay newspaper. One hotel claimed it could not rent them space because it was refinishing its ballroom floors. Finally, CRH booked space at California Hall.

The police were another concern. San Francisco police had a history of harassing gay men, so CRH organizers met with police officials ahead of the event. The police agreed not to interfere. Yet on the night of the ball, officers swarmed the entrance to California

Hall. As more than five hundred guests arrived, including gay men and lesbians and straight clergymen and their wives, the police photographed them. Officers flooded the doorway with the harsh glare of klieg lights and tromped through the dance hall repeatedly to intimidate the crowd. By evening's end, the police had arrested six people, including three lawyers.

The next day, CRH members called a press conference. They blasted the police for the raid and called for an end to police harassment. The press coverage, which was extensive, raised public awareness of police harassment and strengthened gay organizations such as SIR.

The Tenderloin district was not only home to drug pushers and hustlers. It was also home to many drag queens, or men who dress as women. Some drag queens simply like to dress in women's clothing. Others are transsexuals—biological males who feel they are women trapped in male bodies. San Francisco's drag queens weren't welcome much of anywhere in the mid-1960s. But the one place they could always visit was Gene Compton's Cafeteria, which was open twenty-four hours a day. The queens knew they could stop in for a cup of coffee or soup in the wee hours of the morning without being harassed.

Then new managers took over Compton's. They were decidedly less welcoming to the transsexual customers. One night in August 1966, a group of queens became too rowdy for the new management, who called in the police—for the second time that summer.

A police officer grabbed one queen by the arm, but he refused to cooperate. Furious, he threw his cup of coffee in the officer's face. Soon silverware, cups, and plates were whizzing through the air. In an instant, a riot had erupted. The police called for backup while restaurant patrons turned over tables and smashed the restaurant's big glass windows. Before long, the melee had spilled into the street.

"Drag queens beat the police with their heavy purses and kicked them with their high-heeled shoes," writes historian Susan Stryker. When all was said and done, the rioters had burned down a newsstand and vandalized a police car.

AN AMERICAN REVOLUTION

The riot at Compton's was unusual in that it involved drag queens. But across the nation, riots and protests were becoming more and more common. As the 1960s progressed, the United States witnessed more upheaval, more change, and more militancy.

In the early 1960s, the civil rights movement had been characterized by nonviolent protests such as sit-ins. But in the mid-1960s, militant groups such as the Black Panthers joined the peaceful protesters on the civil rights stage.

Thousands of anti-Vietnam War protesters gather in San Francisco, California, in 1967. Protests and riots became more common as change swept the United States in the 1960s.

Women also called for change. Across the country, women began throwing off their aprons and other accessories of motherhood, marriage, and family life. They embraced the women's liberation movement, which sought equal rights and opportunities for women in education, legal matters, and the workforce. With the invention of birth control pills, more women began to have sex outside of marriage. Strict rules about sex and sexuality began to loosen.

By the mid-1960s, the United States was deeply involved in the Vietnam War (1957–1975). Many college students, professors, civil rights activists, and others thought the war was unjust and unnecessary. To protest the war, some young men burned their draft cards, papers that documented their eligibility for military service. Scores of young people participated in antiwar protests. Some protests resulted in violent clashes with the police. In fact, many young people began to think of the police as the enemy during this era. This attitude reflected an overall growing distrust of government and authority on the part of young people.

Some young Americans, dubbed hippies and yippies, embraced a new counterculture. They turned their backs on a traditional life path: marriage, family, a home in the suburbs, and a nine-to-five job with a corporation. Many young men grew their hair long. Both young men and women dressed in colorful clothing, sandals, beads, and headbands, defying the stodgy dress codes of the older generation. Many young people experimented with drugs and had sex with a variety of partners during this era.

As the sixties continued, this new radicalism seemed to be on the rise. And since so many young people were defying authority, dressing flamboyantly, and experimenting with sexual freedom, it was easier for gay people to do so too.

■ THE OSCAR WILDE MEMORIAL BOOKSHOP

Meanwhile, new gay organizations were sprouting up all over the country. They included the Phoenix Society in Kansas City, Missouri; the Dorian Society in Seattle, Washington; and the Promethean Society in Houston, Texas. In New York City, in the fall of 1967, Craig Rodwell realized a long-held dream and opened the first gay bookstore in the United States. The Oscar Wilde Memorial Bookshop, named after an Irish writer who had been imprisoned in the late 1800s for having sex with other men, opened at 291 Mercer Street in Greenwich Village.

Nancy Garden helped Rodwell prepare the shop for its opening. She remembers the store as "a goldmine—what heaven to be able to browse in a shop that specialized in gay books, magazines, newspapers, etc. Suddenly to have 'our' classics and new works available in one friendly, safe place was a terrific gift."

Not everyone welcomed a gay bookstore. Rodwell would come to work to find hateful slurs written on the storefront. He received threatening phone calls, promising harm to him and the store, but the store remained open.

Craig Rodwell stands next to bookshelves at the Oscar Wilde Memorial Bookshop in New York City in 1971. Rodwell opened the shop, which was the first gay bookstore in the United States, in 1967.

◼ GAY IS GOOD

In April 1968, a new play opened to rave reviews Off-Broadway (outside the Broadway theater district). *The Boys in the Band* introduced nine men, eight of whom were gay, celebrating a birthday in a New York City apartment. The characters were largely self-loathing and bitingly funny.

According to critic Clive Barnes, *The Boys in the Band* was "the frankest treatment of homosexuality I have ever seen." "A gem!" said another critic. "An exceptional piece of theater," said another. Clearly, the days of the New York Society for the Suppression of Vice were long gone.

Not everyone liked the play. Frank Kameny hated it. To Kameny, self-loathing had no place in gay culture. Kameny responded with a new creation: a gay slogan.

Other groups had slogans. The radical African American group the Black Panthers, for instance, had coined "Black Is Beautiful." Kameny's slogan, which he introduced at the 1968 North American Conference of Homophile [gay] Organizations, was simply, "Gay Is Good." Not perverted, not sick, not any of the negative things gays had been perceived to be for so long. Not even neutral. *Good*.

CHAPTER 5

THE STONEWALL RIOTS

Gay Power!"

—gay activist Craig Rodwell,
June 28, 1969

Friday night, June 27, 1969, looked to be another lively night at the Stonewall Inn. The jukebox was rocking. The Supremes, Dusty Springfield, and Stevie Wonder were big favorites. The dance floors were jumping, and patrons jammed the booths.

Perhaps nobody was as excited to be there as Steve Ritter, who was celebrating his eighteenth birthday. That made him old enough to legally enter the Stonewall, and he and his best friend, Kiki, had pulled out all the stops. Ritter was decked out in an attractive cocktail dress, stiletto heels, and makeup. So was Kiki. Both had stashed their male clothing in large purses to change into later if necessary. In his women's clothing, Steve Ritter became "Maria" and assumed a female persona.

The Stonewall Inn stood at 53 Christopher Street in Greenwich Village. Built in the late 1800s, it had been a carriage house, a tea-room, and a restaurant before becoming a gay bar. A clutch of streets met just steps from the Stonewall's front door, creating a sort of maze near Sheridan Square. Across the street from the bar was a small park where homeless kids hung out. For some, the park was home.

The Stonewall Inn, shown here in 1969, is a gay bar in Greenwich Village in New York City. The bar was seedy, but it was one of the few places where gay people could socialize and dance together.

The Stonewall's owner in 1969 was a young Mafia member known as Fat Tony. To get around state liquor laws that made it hard to serve gay people, Fat Tony and his associates operated the Stonewall as a private club. The men had no interest in helping gay men socialize. They opened the Stonewall to make money, plain and simple. They cut corners any way they could. The drinks? They watered them down. Inviting decor? Who needed it? Tony painted the walls black and blacked out the windows for privacy. Proper sanitation? Money down the drain. There was no running water behind the bar. When a customer was done with a glass, the bar staff sloshed it through a tub of grimy water before refilling it for the next patron. Bob Kohler, who lived in the neighborhood, called the Stonewall a hellhole. Yet other people considered it home.

The Stonewall drew a cross section of the city's gay population. Most of its clientele were young gay men, though occasionally lesbians dropped in. Queens came to the bar. So did gay street kids. If they could convince the doorman that they were of legal drinking age, they could sit in the Stonewall for hours nursing a drink, away from the cold and hassles of the street.

"The main appeal," notes Kohler, was that the inn "had dancing, which wasn't legally allowed [for same-sex couples] at the time." Customers could dance in either of the inn's two rooms. The front room tended to draw a more staid crowd. The back room, where the music was more raucous and the lighting was dim, was popular with younger patrons.

Craig Rodwell had visited the Stonewall, which was near his apartment, but mostly he avoided it. He loathed Mafia-run gay bars. The Mafia didn't care about gay people. It exploited their legal vulnerability to make money. Anyone who thought otherwise had only to ask the inn's hatcheck girl. She had heard her Mafia managers call the customers every sort of derogatory name in private.

In 1969 a mayoral election was scheduled in New York City. A city election virtually guaranteed that the sitting mayor would order a massive cleanup of the city's streets. The "cleanup" would target drug pushers, prostitutes, and gays. Then the mayor would point to all the

Tommy Lanigan-Schmidt was in his late teens when he left a homophobic (antigay) home life in New Jersey for the streets of New York. "Basically a little group of people hung out in that square that we call Sheridan Square [across from the Stonewall]," he said. "That little group was detested by everyone. I'm telling you, hated, hated, hated because we were kicked out of home. Most of the kids there . . . were . . . thirteen, fourteen. I was like in my late teens.

"Some kids had had boiling water thrown on them by their parents, thrown out through glass doors," he continued. "So we were hanging out together because of what we had in common, which was who hated us, which was everyone as far as we were concerned."

arrests as proof that he was working hard to keep the city respectable. Election time, therefore, was prime time for raiding the city's gay bars.

In June 1969, New York City police officers raided five gay bars within three weeks. On June 24, they raided the Stonewall Inn. This raid was fairly routine. The police entered the bar and arrested staff members while the patrons dispersed and slipped off into the night. As the officers left the bar, though, one of Fat Tony's associates reminded them that the Stonewall would be back up and running the next night. As for the customers, their quiet exit belied their simmering resentment. They were getting fed up with raids.

THE RAID

On Friday night, June 27, Deputy Inspector Seymour Pine of Manhattan's First Division of Public Morals was busy checking details. If everything went according to plan, that night he and his officers would shut down the Stonewall Inn for good.

Pine had laid his plans carefully. He had a slew of search warrants that gave his team the right to confiscate the bar's alcohol and vending machines. The warrants also gave them the right to literally cut apart the wooden bar and haul it off along with the jukebox.

Pine arranged for an array of officers to assist in the raid. Four undercover officers, two male and two female, would enter the Stonewall first. They would scout out ways in which the Stonewall was breaking the law and identify staff members for later arrest. A group of public morals officers, including Detective Charles Smythe, would participate, as would an FBI agent. His job was to check the drinks for their water content. Watering down alcohol was a violation of federal law. Inspector Pine was determined to use every possible legal avenue to close the Stonewall.

Pine gathered his team for a midnight meeting. Soon after, the undercover police officers entered the Stonewall. At around 1:20 A.M. on Saturday morning, Pine led his officers to the Stonewall's imposing front door.

"Police! We're taking the place!" shouted Smythe. The raid was on.

The lights in the bar snapped on, the jukebox fell silent, and the stunned crowd stopped dancing. All talking ceased. In an instant, the police quickly sealed the doors, trapping everyone inside.

Maria Ritter panicked. "I headed for the bathroom, hoping there was a window," she recalled. As she ducked into the ladies' room, a police officer called her back. He grabbed her by the arm and ordered her to stand on one side of the front room.

Michael Fader's reaction was anger. "I just got here and I'm supposed to leave?" he remembered thinking. "I felt myself boiling up inside, getting more and more angry."

The police ordered everyone to line up and produce identification. Officers began herding the bar staff into a back room to process them for arrest. Some officers started seizing the alcohol, while others began ripping the benches from the walls. So far, the raid appeared to be going as planned.

But the mood in the room was edgy. The police literally tearing apart the Stonewall added to the tension. The people lined up along the walls were not feeling cooperative. Some of them talked back to police. Others refused to show identification.

The transvestites, in particular, were not taking the raid quietly. During a typical raid, the transvestites would quickly admit to the police that they were men. But at the Stonewall, they gave the police a lot of trouble. Their behavior was so unruly that Pine decided to arrest them along with the bar staff.

A group of lesbians also gave the police considerable pushback. According to some accounts, when frisking the lesbians, the police had touched them in sexually inappropriate ways.

All in all, it took far longer than usual for the police to line up everyone to check for ID. The wait "felt almost like a hostage situation," remembered Ray Castro. The police "wouldn't answer any questions."

Finally, police began to release customers. Normally, a customer would repocket his or her ID and slip away, anonymity intact. But it was a hot summer night, and the Stonewall had been hopping. That night people lingered.

The small park across from the Stonewall was perfect for gathering. As people collected there, they talked. They talked about recent violence against gay men. They talked about the three gay bars that had been shut down that month. Heterosexuals weren't having their Friday nights ruined by police raids. Why should gay people endure such treatment?

As more and more people filed out of the Stonewall, they joined the growing crowd. People walking by stopped to see what was happening. Before long, well over a hundred people had gathered.

The mood became briefly festive. The crowd cheered as customers exited the Stonewall. The departing customers, in turn, bowed, struck poses, and hammed it up for the onlookers. Then a police wagon drew up to the curb. Inspector Pine had ordered it to hold the confiscated alcohol and additional arrests.

Craig Rodwell and Fred Sargeant were walking home to Craig's apartment when they came upon the scene. Another raid, they guessed, but this one, with its restless gathering, was different. They sought out the tallest stoop in the area to watch the action.

With the arrival of the police wagon, Inspector Pine exited the Stonewall. As far as he was concerned, the raid was just about over. All he had to do was load the wagon. Then he saw the crowd. Undaunted, Pine proceeded to help load the wagon with the Mafia members and then the bartenders and other staff.

Craig Rodwell watched, furious. Suddenly, he let out a yell: "Gay Power!"

His cry rang out into the night, and a few people repeated it. Others just giggled.

The police then loaded the transvestites into the wagon. When one officer shoved a queen, she slugged him with her purse. He whacked her with his nightstick. Watching this scene, the crowd began to boo and beat the wagon. If the police were shoving queens in full view of the crowd, what were they doing to people still in the bar? Beating them up? The crowd began pelting the police vehicles with pennies.

"In one second, what was very festive turned ugly and nasty," said Bob Kohler, who had been out walking his dog. "There was a lot of confusion, a lot of screaming."

The police ordered the crowd to move back, but they refused. Someone threw a beer can, which hit the patrol wagon. "Get the Mafia out of the bars!" yelled Rodwell.

All this time, Maria Ritter had been held inside the Stonewall. Then the police steered her outside toward the wagon. Ritter was terrified. Jail was a notoriously dangerous place for transsexuals, who risked being raped by other prisoners.

She went into the wagon "with a whole group of older drag queens," she remembers, "and I'm thinking to myself, I'm *dead*." When the police opened the doors to load more prisoners, Ritter slipped out. A police officer tried to stop her, but Ritter pleaded with him. "Please! It's my birthday! I'm eighteen. And my mother's going to kill me." The cop quietly let her go.

The police were not so forgiving with a furious, solidly built lesbian whom they tried to force into a squad car. She was in handcuffs, arrested for failing to wear the required three pieces of female clothing. Every time the police managed to shove her into the squad car, she fought her way out and tried to run into the Stonewall.

Police push back the angry crowd outside the Stonewall on June 28, 1969.

For the onlookers, the woman's struggle was the last straw. One bystander picked up a loose cobblestone and heaved it all the way across Christopher Street at the squad car. It hit the hood with frightening force.

Soon people were flinging bottles and bricks against the front of the Stonewall. The police in the wagon and squad cars prepared to leave. Pine, alarmed at the crowd's size and fury, urged the drivers to drop the prisoners off at the Sixth Precinct Station as quickly as possible and hurry back. The vehicles set off slowly through the angry throng, their sirens wailing.

The crowd continued to launch bottles, cans, and coins. The situation was so volatile that Pine ordered all his officers into the Stonewall for safety. Howard Smith, a reporter with the *Village Voice*, had just arrived on the scene, and he sought cover with the police. Once inside, the police barricaded the doors with chairs and tables.

Their retreat seemed to spur the crowd on even more. The torrent of bricks, bottles, and cobblestones intensified. Soon someone heaved a wire mesh garbage can through a window of the Stonewall. It hit its mark, shattering the glass. With savage effort, a few men yanked a parking meter from the pavement and used it as a battering ram. They rammed the big front door of the Stonewall over and over.

Then Craig Rodwell's battle cry caught on. "Gay Power!" the crowd yelled, no longer self-conscious or uncertain. "Gay Power!"

The police huddled inside the Stonewall listened anxiously as bricks and stones rained down on the building. Someone was pounding the door with something huge. The crowd, wrote Howard Smith, sounded "like a powerful rage bent on vendetta [revenge]."

Craig Rodwell surveyed the scene from the vantage point of the stoop. Here "was the spark we had been waiting for for years," he realized. But it would mean little if nobody knew about it. He and Sargeant quickly sought out pay telephones and notified the press.

Some in the crowd began to throw Molotov cocktails—homemade explosives fashioned out of bottles and gasoline—into the bar. The police inside quickly used up the contents of the fire extinguisher to put out the resulting flames. They were unable to call for help because their radios failed to work and someone had cut the phone lines. They could hardly send someone out the front door for aid—the crowd was too dangerous. It looked as if they would all die, engulfed in flames at the Stonewall Inn.

A few officers, desperate, pulled their guns. Pine, as tense as he was, realized the guns spelled new trouble. He realized that if one officer fired a shot, it would set off the rest of them. He managed, just barely, to keep the officers calm by speaking to each person one on one. The smaller of the two policewomen escaped the building by crawling through a small opening near the roof. Avoiding Christopher Street, she rushed to a nearby fire station for help.

In the crowd outside, Morty Manford remembered, "People took a garbage can, one of those wire mesh cans, and set it on fire and threw the burning garbage into the premises. The area that was set afire is where the coatroom was." Next, someone outside reached into a window, squirted a liquid into the room, and tossed in a lit match.

Just then, sirens sounded. Two fire engines arrived, plus a patrol wagon and more police. As the new forces pushed back the crowd, Pine and the rest of the group were able to walk out of the Stonewall.

Two buses pulled up carrying twenty-four members of the city's Tactical Patrol Force (TPF). The TPF, equipped with riot gear, "lived to break heads," said one witness. Wearing helmets and carrying riot shields, the TPF assembled into a V-shaped formation and began to march down Christopher Street, splitting up the crowd.

But the mazelike streets worked in the crowd's favor. The TPF "would chase us down the street," said Rodwell, "and we'd just go around the block and come back and chant things and throw bottles." The gay men "owned" these streets, and they were not about to let the TPF chase them from the one scrap of turf they claimed as theirs.

YVONNE RITTER REMEMBERS

Steve Ritter (also known as Maria) "knew from an early age that I was a girl." In 1969 her "gender dysphoria [unhappiness] was [considered] a psychiatric illness," she said. But Ritter did not think she was crazy. "When I found gay people, I thought I had died and gone to heaven," Ritter continued. "Because these are people who accepted me for who I was, let me dress the way I wanted to."

Ritter barely escaped arrest during the Stonewall riots. "I didn't return the next night because I figured I got away by the skin of my teeth," she said. "But I sat home, and I said, there's something about this. This is going to be really, really significant in history." Eventually Ritter transitioned surgically from male to female and changed her first name to Yvonne.

A group of gay street kids, including some effeminate-looking youths, had their own way of dealing with the TPF. Says one witness, "These queens all of a sudden rolled up their pant legs into knickers." Gathering dangerously close to the police, they formed a kick line, in the style of the famous dance group the Rockettes, and began to sing:

> We are the Stonewall girls
> We wear our hair in curls
> We wear our dungarees
> Above our nelly [feminine] knees

Twice, three times, they ran around the block, reassembling their kick line for the advancing TPF. Finally, said Danny Garvin, "the cops just charged [with their nightsticks] and started smacking them in the heads."

Eventually the crowd began to disperse. By dawn the riot had ebbed. Left in its wake were a few bleeding street kids, small groups of police, and the wrecked front windows of the Stonewall Inn. Burning trash cans, set alight by the rioters, crackled quietly up and down the street.

When police raided the Stonewall, they tore apart the bar, including the booths and the jukebox. A fire on the first night of rioting did even more damage.

The riot had begun in an instant, completely unplanned. And who had the toughest fighters been? The young queens, the transvestites, and the angry lesbians who fought the police. "It is as if on the morning of June 28, 1969," wrote historian David Carter, "America symbolically got back the anger she had created by her neglect of her most despised children: the fairies, queens and nelly boys she had so utterly abandoned."

■ ■ ■ ■ DAY TWO

By the next day, the windows of the Stonewall Inn were boarded up. People had scrawled messages on its walls: "Legalize Gay Bars!" "Support Gay Power!"

News of the riots had spread through word of mouth as well as newspaper and radio reports. Throughout the day, people drifted to Christopher Street, curious to see the damage from the night's unrest. Many of them lingered, and as day turned to evening, a crowd formed. By midnight, on one of the summer's hottest nights, hundreds of the city's gay men and lesbians had congregated in the streets around the Stonewall Inn. When the police tried to move them along, they chanted slogans in reply. "Equality for homosexuals!" "Liberate Christopher Street!" they shouted, their anger building.

Once again, Craig Rodwell was there. The crowds were so immense that Rodwell and some others decided to simply block off Christopher Street with their bodies and declare it a gays-only zone. Let the heterosexuals see what it was like to be shut out for a change.

Friday night's rioting had erupted suddenly. Saturday night was different: the crowd was bigger, its anger more focused, its reason for being there absolutely deliberate. It was there in the name of gay power.

"We were just out. We were in the streets. I mean, can you imagine?" said Chris Babick. Rather than "disappear into this cavern, this place called the Stonewall," here was "the homosexual man standing on the streets. And it was incredible."

Violence erupted once more, and another night of rioting ensued. Rioters threw bottles, rocked passing cars and taxis, and even attacked police cars. The police, in turn, were seen flailing furiously at rioters with their nightsticks. Just after two at night, 150 members of the TPF arrived in riot gear to clear Christopher Street.

At the top of the street, the TPF formed a solid line, shoulder to shoulder. Each man held an immense plastic shield, so the force looked like a huge plastic wall topped by a series of blue helmets. In this fearsome formation, the TPF began to march slowly and menacingly down Christopher Street. At the point where Christopher Street met Waverly Place, the TPF once again met young queens in kick-line formation.

They again launched into their Stonewall song: "We are the Stonewall girls / We wear our hair in curls . . . ." As the city's most intimidating force advanced, the queens held their ground. The TPF got all of 8 feet (2.4 meters) away before the "Stonewall girls" finally fled— temporarily. They dashed through the mazelike streets and reassembled their kick line for the TPF.

The TPF took on rioters throughout the neighborhood. Witnesses saw one TPF officer come up behind one man and crack open his head with a nightstick.

By three thirty, the crowds had scattered, leaving the streets to the TPF, which lingered even later into the night. The second night of the Stonewall riots was over.

■ ■ ■ "NOTHING'S GOING TO BE THE SAME"

The two nights of rioting prompted different responses among New York City's gay leaders. "Everybody sensed that nothing's going to be the same after this," said Craig Rodwell. And if the riots marked a turning point, Rodwell wasn't about to let it pass without using it to mobilize the gay community.

Early Sunday morning, Rodwell wrote a leaflet. The nights of the riots, he wrote, "will go down in history as the first time that thousands of Homosexual men and women went into the streets to protest the intolerable situation which has existed in New York City for many years." He urged gay businesspeople to open bars to replace the Mafia-run bars. Rodwell used his own money to print thousands

After the riots, members of the Mattachine Society wrote a message on the Stonewall Inn. They asked for help in keeping the streets of Greenwich Village "peaceful and quiet."

of copies of the leaflet and arranged for teams of workers to distribute them on Sunday afternoon throughout Greenwich Village.

The leaders of New York's Mattachine Society, on the other hand, were troubled by the riots. Dick Leitsch, head of Mattachine, felt the riots gave the impression that gay people were a bunch of screaming queens, not respectable citizens who just happened to be attracted to members of their own sex. The society posted a sign on the Stonewall that urged, "Please help maintain peaceful and quiet conduct on the streets of the Village." Yet Leitsch also recognized the opportunity the riots presented. In an article titled "The Hairpin Drop Heard Around the World," he characterized the Stonewall riots as "the opening shot" in a new push for gay rights.

THE LAST NIGHT

The area around the Stonewall Inn was fairly quiet the next few nights, mostly because of rain. Then came Wednesday. That day the *Village Voice* carried two front-page stories about the weekend's riots. The *Voice*, with offices close to the Stonewall, had always positioned itself as the city's hip, progressive newspaper—except when it came to gay life. Its editors took pains to distance themselves from the gay community, a policy that had "long infuriated most homosexuals," noted Dick Leitsch. The paper's Stonewall articles used derogatory phrases to describe the rioters. Some members of the gay community wanted to burn down the newspaper's offices. Instead, they took to the streets again.

That night they had company. Rioters representing a cross section of the city's radical groups, including the Black Panthers, yippies, and members of street gangs from as far away as New Jersey, joined the riot. They apparently were drawn not by a new allegiance to the gay movement. Rather, they were impressed that "these were the only

A crowd gathers on Christopher Street on July 2, 1969—the last night of rioting in Greenwich Village, New York City. Police officers keep an eye on the crowd from across the street.

> "In 1969, I was fourteen years old, growing up in the New York City borough [section] of Queens. News of the Stonewall riots just barely reached me, and the idea of gay and lesbian people screaming for their rights was a little bit scary but eye-opening at the same time. It was the start of something big for the world and certainly for me as well. . . . Anyone who grows up gay, lesbian, bisexual, or transgendered can't help being aware of a painful lack of role models and what a critical role is played by the few we have. For me, those fuzzy and distant images of the rioters at Stonewall were an inspiration through my teenage years and the rest of my life."
>
> —Thomas Duane, New York state senator, 1999

rioters that had gotten the best of the police," said Bob Kohler. In previous years, the police had put down uprisings by some of the most radical groups, such as the Students for a Democratic Society. In all those incidents, Kohler noted, "police were never put on the run, and suddenly they were put on the run by the [gay men], so those people were very curious: did this really happen?"

The rioting on Wednesday lasted less than two hours, but it was some of the most intense of the entire week. All patience on both sides had run out. There were no silly kick lines. The police used their nightsticks at the slightest provocation.

By the time order was restored, "young people, many of them queens, were lying on the sidewalk, bleeding from the head, face, mouth, and even the eyes," said Dick Leitsch. At least one police officer was injured as well.

The Stonewall riots were over. The change they inspired, however, was just beginning.

CHAPTER 6

EUPHORIC
1969–1970

"And we are euphoric, high, with the initial flourish of a movement."

—Carl Wittman, "A Gay Manifesto," 1969

The shards of glass had barely been swept from Christopher Street when Craig Rodwell boarded a charter bus for Philadelphia, Pennsylvania, on the morning of July 4. It was time for the Annual Reminder, the yearly picket in front of Independence Hall. Rodwell had recruited a large number of picketers. They set out from New York City, buzzing about the Stonewall riots.

The 1969 Annual Reminder drew seventy-five picketers, its biggest turnout yet. Longtime leaders such as Frank Kameny and Barbara Gittings were there, as well as many new, younger participants. The Annual Reminder began with the picketers marching silently in single file, holding their signs. But much had changed since the first Annual Reminder in 1965. Much had changed in the previous *week*. It was hardly surprising, then, that two young women in front of Rodwell did the unthinkable: they held hands.

Rodwell thought their quiet display of affection was wonderful. Not so Frank Kameny. He quickly broke them up. "None of that!" he ordered. From the earliest pickets, he had insisted that picketers not make onlookers uncomfortable by putting gay romance on show.

Hearing Kameny's comment, Rodwell completely lost his patience. A new day called for new tactics. He urged the couples from New York to hold hands. Barging up to Kameny and two journalists, he launched into an impassioned outburst about Stonewall and what it meant. He insisted that gay people had the right to do all the things straight people did, including holding hands. Rodwell's rant did not go over well with Kameny, but it suited the younger picketers perfectly.

On the bus ride back to New York City, Rodwell realized they had just staged the last Annual Reminder. It was obvious that the staid pickets of the 1960s were over. Yet he felt wistful. He valued these opportunities to march in the name of gay rights. Then he hit on an idea: why not initiate a new event to commemorate the Stonewall riots, an event that embraced a new gay activism? Rodwell even thought of a name: Christopher Street Liberation Day.

■ ■ ■ GAY LIBERATION FRONT

Mattachine New York called a meeting for July 16 to organize around gay liberation. Dick Leitsch, in a brown suit, tried to lead the meeting of two hundred people. Acceptance of gays and lesbians would take time, he explained. "We don't want acceptance!" shouted a young man named Jim Fouratt. "We have got to radicalize, man!"

Fouratt and like-minded activists, mostly young and new to the movement, had no time for patience. Many already had worked for radical causes, such as the movement against the war in Vietnam. They sought to build on the energy of the riots to forge fast, dramatic change. By the end of July, they had formed a new organization: the Gay Liberation Front (GLF). The word *liberation* was loaded with meaning. Women's liberation meant throwing off the shackles imposed by society, the stifling gender roles and expectations, and living one's life fully, without limits. Now gays and lesbians were declaring their liberation.

GLF members immediately ran into conflict over what purpose the group should serve. Many of them insisted that GLF join forces with other radical groups. GLF, they asserted, had to join the larger revolution against "the establishment." It should work with the Black Panthers and fight for migrant farmworkers in California, they argued, and for the war-torn Vietnamese, the poor, and the oppressed.

Other members of GLF felt strongly that the organization would be more effective if it focused solely on gay issues. Furthermore, they doubted that other radical groups would offer their support. For instance, Eldridge Cleaver of the Black Panthers had said, "Homosexuality is a sickness," like "baby-rape." It made no sense to many in the GLF to join forces with anyone homophobic.

GLF meetings tended to be chaotic, with a lot of shouting. Members hell-bent on radical change demeaned those with a less ambitious agenda, and many of the young, radical members had no use for the "old guard" 1960s activists or respect for what they had accomplished. When Frank Kameny and Barbara Gittings attended a GLF meeting, one member demanded, "What are your credentials?"

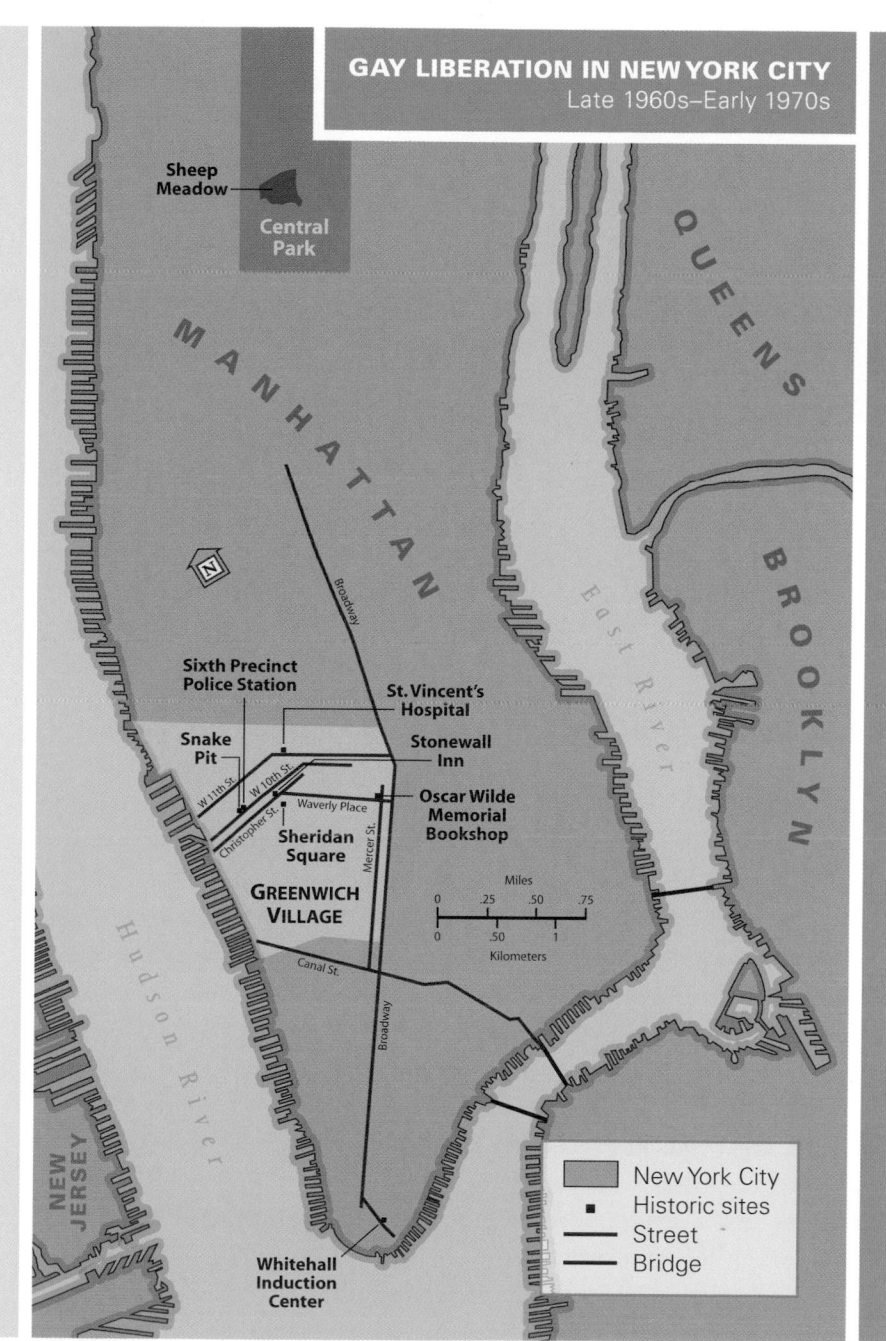

GAY LIBERATION IN NEW YORK CITY
Late 1960s–Early 1970s

Sheep Meadow

Central Park

MANHATTAN

QUEENS

BROOKLYN

Broadway

Sixth Precinct Police Station

St. Vincent's Hospital

Snake Pit

Stonewall Inn

W 11th St.

W 10th St.

Waverly Place

Oscar Wilde Memorial Bookshop

Christopher St.

Sheridan Square

Mercer St.

GREENWICH VILLAGE

East River

Miles
0   .25   .50   .75
0   .50   1
Kilometers

Hudson River

Canal St.

Broadway

New York City

Historic sites

Street

Bridge

NEW JERSEY

Whitehall Induction Center

Members of the Gay Liberation Front attend a meeting in New York City in 1970. The GLF wanted to take radical action for gay rights.

Whatever the GLF's shortcomings, it was instrumental in taking the raw energy released by the Stonewall riots and forging the next wave of gay activism. What's more, the GLF introduced dances—the first "gay dances by gay people for gay people, with the money that was handed in at the door going to gay issues and gay causes," remembers Bob Kohler. Lesbians could dance with lesbians, and gay men with gay men. Added Kohler, "This was a fabulous first."

■ THE GAY ACTIVISTS ALLIANCE

Marty Robinson attended some GLF meetings in 1969. While he appreciated the group's militancy, he disagreed with its multi-issue approach. Robinson wanted to focus only on gay issues and so did a number of other GLF members. In November 1969, they broke off to form a new group: the Gay Activists Alliance (GAA).

GAA, under the leadership of Robinson, Arthur Evans, Arthur Bell, Jim Owles, and Kay Tobin, took a radical, activist approach but one that embraced order over chaos. The group created a formal constitution spelling out its beliefs and aims. It adopted a logo, the lambda, a Greek letter that resembles an upside-down Y.

GAA members began putting pressure on New York's elected officials to endorse gay rights. One of their chief targets was Mayor John Lindsay. In March 1970, GAA activists staged a boisterous picket on New York City Hall but were unable to secure a meeting with the mayor.

Soon after the police raided a gay bar called the Snake Pit. Deputy Inspector Seymour Pine, who had led the raid on the Stonewall, was again in charge. As the raid progressed, people leaving the Snake Pit began congregating outside. When Pine saw the crowd gathering, he feared another riot was brewing and decided to arrest everyone left in the bar. He and his officers rounded up more than 160 people and transported them to the Sixth Precinct Station.

One of the men in custody was Diego Vinales, an Argentine with an expired visa. Therefore, he no longer had permission to live in the United States. He was so terrified of being deported (sent back to his home country) for being gay that he made a desperate attempt at escape. He tried to jump from an upper window of the police station to the roof of an adjacent building.

He missed. He fell through the gap between buildings and wound up impaled on six 14-inch-long (35-centimeter) spikes of an iron fence. Firefighters had to remove part of the fence with an electric saw before they could transport Vinales to the hospital.

The incident enraged activists. Within a matter of hours, GAA had planned a protest march for the following night. Members made phone calls, alerted the press, and distributed a pamphlet. "Any way you look at it—that boy was PUSHED!!" Robinson wrote. "We are ALL being pushed."

In 1970 there was no Internet, cell phones, or Twitter. Yet word of the march spread quickly. That night hundreds of protesters, gay and straight, marched from Christopher Street to the Sixth Precinct (police) Station. As they marched, they chanted, "Say it loud: gay is proud!" They continued on to St. Vincent's Hospital, where Vinales lay in a coma. They lit candles outside the hospital in support of his recovery. That so many people turned out—and on such short notice—illustrated the progress the gay rights movement had made since the Stonewall riots.

YOU'VE BEEN ZAPPED!

The sunny morning of April 13, 1970, marked the one-hundredth birthday of the Metropolitan Museum of Art in New York City. A throng of well-wishers had turned out to celebrate. Mayor John Lindsay climbed the museum's steps at 9:55 to address the gathering. He joked congenially with the museum's leaders and lavished thanks on the wealthy donor who had funded the museum's new plaza. Everything seemed to be going swimmingly.

WHY THE **LAMBDA**?

No one knows for certain why the GAA chose the lambda symbol (below). Some people say it is an L for "liberation." Others note that the lambda is the symbol for energy in chemistry and physics and thus denotes energy in the gay rights movement. Regardless of its meaning, it has endured as a symbol of the gay rights movement.

Then a young man in a baseball jacket seized the microphone. "When are you going to speak out on homosexual rights, Mr. Mayor?" demanded GAA's Marty Robinson.

"The demonstrator was promptly hustled off by two crash-helmeted police," reported the *New York Times*. But other GAA members had infiltrated the crowd. They handed out leaflets that said, "Why can't a 'Gay' be Mayor?" They joined the receiving line to shake the mayor's hand, each one questioning him on his support for gay rights. Jim Owles pressed a leaflet into his hand. "You have our leaflet," said Owles. "Now when the hell are you going to speak to homosexuals?"

Mayor Lindsay had just been "zapped." The zap, a form of direct political action, put a person of influence on the spot in a public confrontation on the issue of gay rights.

GAA members became masters of the zap. When Lindsay failed to respond to requests for a meeting, GAA continued to zap him. It also zapped *Harper's* magazine after it published an insulting article about gay people. It zapped Fidelifacts when it learned the data-collection agency sold information about people's sexuality to prospective employers. It zapped elected city officials who turned a deaf ear to gay rights. Zaps proved to be an effective tactic for putting the issue of gay rights in the public spotlight.

■ THE LAVENDER MENACE

Activist lesbians in those years often felt torn. Many were not only gay, they were feminists as well. But organizations such as GLF had a predominantly male membership and tended to focus on issues important to gay men. Meanwhile, many feminist organizations wanted nothing to do with lesbians. Betty Friedan, the head of the National Organization of Women (NOW), called lesbians "the lavender menace." (The color lavender was a symbol of homosexuality.) Lesbian involvement, she claimed, would hurt the movement's reputation. When NOW held its first Congress to Unite Women in November 1969, it did not include the Daughters of Bilitis on its list of sponsors.

In April 1970, Clive Barnes, the theater critic for the *New York Times*, made a return visit to the Off-Broadway production of *The Boys in the Band*. Two years earlier, he had declared the play about a group of gay men to be groundbreaking. "Hilariously funny, ineffably [indescribably] sad," another critic had raved.

But this time something was different. "The damnedest thing has happened to it," Barnes wrote in his review. "[The play] has become a period piece." Two years—including three days of riots—had yielded a torrent of changes in the gay community. The "ineffably sad" homosexuals of the 1960s had given way to the liberated gay men and lesbians of the 1970s.

Something had to give. "We knew we would no longer accept second-class status in the women's movement or the gay movement," wrote Karla Jay. "We would be equal partners, or we would leave the straight women and gay men behind."

Rita Mae Brown, a GLF member, started holding consciousness-raising sessions for GLF's lesbian members. At these sessions, the women worked to better understand their identities as lesbians and feminists. Brown, Jay, and a number of other women wrote "The Woman-Identified Woman." This ten-paragraph manifesto argued that lesbians, having lived their lives outside societal norms, were naturally suited to serve at the forefront of the women's liberation movement.

The women hatched a plan to challenge NOW's anti-lesbianism.

NOW would sponsor the second Congress to Unite Women in early May 1970. Ahead of the meeting, the GLF women hand-dyed T-shirts in a bathtub. They silk-screened each T-shirt with the words *Lavender Menace*.

On the evening of May 1, three hundred women gathered in a Manhattan auditorium for NOW's Congress to Unite Women. The first speaker was about to address the group when the lights went out. The microphone went dead. Suddenly, up went the lights, and there in the aisles stood nearly twenty women wearing Lavender Menace T-shirts. They held placards with messages such as "Take a Lesbian to Lunch!" They handed out copies of "The Woman-Identified Woman" and took to the stage. They addressed the audience, insisting that lesbians be heard and be made part of the feminist movement. While NOW's leadership was peeved, the audience was supportive. Ultimately, NOW passed a set of pro-lesbian resolutions.

Rita Mae Brown *(right)* and other GLF members confronted NOW's Congress to Unite Women in 1970. The activists wanted the women's liberation movement to embrace lesbian involvement.

■ ■ ■ PLANNING

Craig Rodwell had a lot of work to do to make Christopher Street Liberation Day (CSLD) a reality. He sent notices to New York's gay organizations, asking them to send representatives to CSLD committee meetings. Rodwell also organized some of his bookstore customers to help.

Starting in February 1970, a group of around eight people began to meet monthly at Rodwell's apartment to hammer out details. Would Christopher Street Liberation Day be a two-day festival or simply a march? A march. Well, then, what would the route be? What staff and city permits would they need?

The march, they decided, would start in midtown Manhattan and end in Central Park's Sheep Meadow, where marchers would hold a "gay-in." They contacted gay and lesbian groups around the country, encouraging them to hold similar celebrations in their own cities. They asked for donations, but the take was discouraging. By April seven groups had sent in a grand total of just one hundred dollars. When Rodwell found a twenty-dollar bill on the street, he decided, "God has sent it for the march."

■ ■ ■ JUNE 28, 1970

At one on Sunday afternoon, June 28, Craig Rodwell studied the crowd gathering on Waverly Street in Greenwich Village for the Christopher Street Liberation Day march. Months of planning had gone into this day. The CSLD committee had held countless meetings.

Just an hour before the scheduled kickoff, dozens of police officers were on hand. But marchers? At most, one thousand people had shown up. True, one thousand marchers would constitute the largest organized demonstration of gay people in U.S. history. But only one thousand? After all those notices? In a city with so many gay people?

Maybe, despite all that had happened in the previous year, the old fears of harassment and violence were as strong as ever. Already, someone had pelted some marchers with eggs from an upstairs apartment window. Some gay people stood on the sidewalk, hanging back, looking indecisive. Maybe they would march. Maybe they would not.

Around a quarter after two, the march began. The people in front carried a banner reading, "Christopher Street Gay Liberation Day 1970." Another marcher carried a U.S. flag. Approximately two hundred GAA members marched in blue T-shirts emblazoned with gold lambdas. They held up their fingers in the *V* for "victory" sign and marched up Sixth Avenue. They chanted, "Two, four, six, eight / Gay is just as good as straight!" and "Out of the closets and into the streets!" They hoisted signs and banners: "Gay Pride," "Lesbians Unite," "New York Mattachine." Dressed in a neat casual shirt and slacks, Frank Kameny carried a sign saying, "GAY IS GOOD."

Participants in the Christopher Street Gay Liberation Day march on June 28, 1970, carry banners celebrating gay pride.

Maria Ritter, who had nearly been arrested the night of the Stonewall riots, decided to march at the last minute. Coming in from Brooklyn, she rushed uptown, seeking the marchers. "As she rounded the corner approaching Macy's department store . . . there they were— placards and banners waving bravely in the sun," wrote historian Martin Duberman.

As the marchers headed north, their numbers steadily swelled. People joined in midway, stepping off sidewalks into the street. The marchers, then numbering about ten thousand, filled fifteen city blocks.

The violence many had feared never materialized, though the marchers drew plenty of stares. "Wondrous faces poked out of air-conditioned cars," reported the *Village Voice*, marveling at the scene.

The march ended at the Sheep Meadow in Central Park, a grassy area just over a bluff. There marchers joined the gay-in, a huge gathering of people basking in the freedom of just being themselves, out in the open. They applauded new arrivals coming over the hill. "No one had ever seen so many homosexuals in one place before," noted authors Dudley Clendinen and Adam Nagourney. "On top of the bluff, many of these men and women, who had grown up so isolated and alone, stood in silence and cried."

Others laughed with delight. "Would you believe it! It's a gay Woodstock!" said one man, referring to the 1969 music festival in upstate New York that had drawn more than four hundred thousand hippies. "And after all those years I spent in psychotherapy!"

"What will your shrink [psychiatrist] do without you?" his friend replied, laughing. "He's dependent on you for the payments on his car."

■ ■ ■ CHRISTOPHER STREET WEST

On the same day in Los Angeles, gays and lesbians honored Stonewall's anniversary with a parade down Hollywood Boulevard. The event, sponsored by the GLF and the Metropolitan Community Church (MCC, a gay Christian congregation), drew about twelve hundred people, some on floats, representing thirty different organizations.

Initially, the Los Angeles police had tried to prevent the march. "Granting a permit to a group of homosexuals to parade down Hollywood Boulevard would be the same as giving a permit to a group of thieves and murderers!" said the LA police chief. But the marchers finally obtained a permit through a court order.

Said MCC founder Troy Perry, "We made up our minds that year to show our pride with parades and demonstrations. And we've never looked back."

THE **METROPOLITAN COMMUNITY CHURCH**

From the time he was a kid, Troy Perry (below, in 1971) felt a calling to preach. He preached at one church and then another. Both kicked him out upon learning that he was gay, but Perry's calling remained. On October 6, 1968, he led a worship service for a dozen gay men in his home near Los Angeles.

That first service grew into the Metropolitan Community Church. MCC has grown to include 250 congregations in twenty-three countries.

CHAPTER 7

HOPE
THE
SEVENTIES

And you and you and you,
you have to give people hope."

—Harvey Milk, San Francisco city supervisor
and gay rights advocate, March 10, 1978

During the early 1970s, it seemed the tide was truly starting to turn in the struggle for gay equality. In the wake of the Stonewall riots, the number of gay and lesbian organizations could no longer be counted on one or two hands. Hundreds of such organizations formed across the country. The greater involvement began to yield new milestones. For instance:

- In May 1971, the hit television show *All in the Family* introduced a gay character: a tough, masculine man who did not hide his homosexuality from bigoted Archie Bunker.

- In 1972 East Lansing, Michigan, became the first city to pass an ordinance banning discrimination in hiring based on sexual orientation.

- Jim Foster, a cofounder of SIR in San Francisco, became the first openly gay person to speak at a presidential convention with his address to the 1972 Democratic National Convention.

- In January 1974, Kathy Kozachenko became the first openly gay candidate to win political office when she was elected to the city council in Ann Arbor, Michigan.

In 1974 Elaine Noble became the first openly gay person elected to a state office when she won a seat in the Massachusetts House of Representatives. "It was a very ugly campaign," Noble remembered. People shot bullets through her windows, destroyed her car, and broke the windows at her campaign headquarters. After taking office, she said, "I had to deal with human feces left in my desk and a lot of obscene profanities. I just tried to maintain with what level of dignity that I could."

The courts were handling more gay rights cases, too. In Minnesota in 1970, two gay men, Jack Baker and James Michael McConnell, applied for a marriage license. The state refused to issue one, although nothing in the law specified that the state could grant licenses only to opposite-sex couples. The men sued. Their case, *Baker v. Nelson*, though not successful, was the first legal challenge to the prohibition of same-sex marriages. When a Washington State school system fired a teacher for being gay, he filed a lawsuit, *Gaylord v. Tacoma*. Here again, the court ruled against the gay plaintiff. Yet these cases inspired other gay people to file lawsuits and brought increased public attention to the issue of gay rights.

■ ■ ■ "THE GREATEST MASS CURE"

In 1970 the American Psychiatric Association held a convention in San Francisco. During one session, a psychiatrist addressed his colleagues on aversion therapy for gay men. The therapy involved giving patients electric shocks and nausea-inducing drugs.

During the talk, people suddenly began to yell. "Where did you take your residency [medical training]—*Auschwitz?*" someone shouted, referring to the World War II concentration camp where guards, under orders from the German government, tortured and killed Jewish prisoners. Another GAA zap was under way.

GAA members had slipped into the audience. Planted throughout the room, they heckled the speaker, infuriating the psychiatrists. "Maniac!" one of them yelled at a GAA member. Before the session ended, the police, guns drawn, had arrived on the scene. But one psychiatrist, Kent Robinson, agreed to seat gay spokespeople on a panel at the APA convention the following year.

At the 1971 convention in Washington, D.C., Frank Kameny, Barbara Gittings, Del Martin, Lilli Vincenz, and Jack Baker made up that panel. It would be the first time gay people had addressed the APA on the issue of homosexuality.

To cover all bases, though, GAA planned a major zap. It would invade the convention during the keynote address, and GAA's spokesperson would take over the microphone. Members planned the zap for weeks, studying diagrams of the hotel, identifying all the fire doors, and learning their way around the woods that surrounded the hotel. The day of the keynote address, a few GAA members would slip into the room with the psychiatrists. Then, on cue, they would open the fire doors for other GAA members waiting outside.

Zap Day arrived. While approximately two thousand psychiatrists listened to the keynote address, thirty activists burst into the hall through the fire doors. By accident, the GAA spokesperson ended up locked out of the room. Without hesitation, Frank Kameny climbed over the edge of the stage and rushed to the podium. The stunned moderator asked him what he was doing.

"I'm seizing the microphone!" said Kameny. He proceeded to attack the psychiatric profession for the harm it had done to gay people. Later, he spoke as part of the panel. "The person who *really* needs the psychotherapy," he said, ". . . is not the homosexual youngster who gets *dragged* into a psychiatrist's office by his mother, but the mother, to relieve her anxieties about his homosexuality."

The 1972 APA convention was in Dallas, Texas. Barbara Gittings had learned that unknown to most of the association, the APA membership included a sizable contingent of gay psychiatrists. They kept their sexuality a secret from their colleagues and patients. They even had their own secret society, which they covertly referred to as the Gay-PA. After much searching, Gittings had found a gay psychiatrist willing to address his colleagues. He asked only that his identity remain a secret.

Thus a Dr. H. Anonymous (H for "homosexual") joined Gittings and Kameny on the 1972 panel discussion "Psychiatry: Friend or Foe to the Homosexuals?" The gay psychiatrist appeared in a large distorted mask, a wig, and an oversized tuxedo. Dr. Anonymous explained to his colleagues that more than two hundred gay psychiatrists were attending the convention. He spoke of the burden of their double lives. His presentation was so powerful that his colleagues gave him a standing ovation.

On December 15, 1973, the board of trustees of the APA voted unanimously to remove homosexuality from its list of mental illnesses. What's more, the APA spoke out publicly against all forms of discrimination based on sexual orientation. "It was probably

Left to right: **Barbara Gittings, Frank Kameny, and "Dr. H. Anonymous" sit on a panel at the 1972 American Psychiatric Association convention in Dallas, Texas. Dr. Anonymous was a gay psychiatrist who helped convince the group to change its view of homosexuality as a mental illness.**

the greatest mass cure in the history of medicine," wrote authors Dudley Clendinen and Adam Nagourney in *Out for Good.*

■ A SERGEANT COMES OUT

Leonard Matlovich knew from the time he was twelve that he was gay. For years he struggled with his identity. As a kid, he prayed on his knees in his room, asking God to change him. He joined the air force as soon as he could, welcoming the order he found there and hoping his attraction to other men would end. He served with distinction in Vietnam once, twice, and three times and was blown up by a land mine in the Vietnamese city of Da Nang. The pain he felt afterward, he realized, paled in comparison to the pain he felt over his sexuality.

In 1972, at Eglin Air Force Base in Florida, Matlovich came close to committing suicide. He had a gun to his temple when he heard a scratching at the door. Ralph, his dog, wanted in. Ralph, a happy mutt adopted from the shelter, sensed something was wrong. He refused to leave, and Matlovich decided to persevere.

At the age of thirty, Matlovich finally accepted his sexuality. He knew that it had had no bearing on his performance in the military. He had a perfect military record and had received two medals. Matlovich believed the ban on gays in the military was simply wrong. When he saw Frank Kameny's name in a military magazine, he flew to Washington to meet with him. Kameny had been looking for a member of the military to file a test case challenging the ban, and Matlovich eagerly volunteered.

On March 6, 1975, he gave his superior officer at Langley Air Force Base a letter. "I have arrived at the conclusion that my sexual preferences are homosexual," he stated. "I have also concluded that my sexual preferences will in no way interfere with my Air Force duties." He asked the air force to waive its policy and allow him to continue serving his country.

Leonard Matlovich holds his discharge papers from the air force in 1975. Matlovich decided to challenge the ban on gays in the military in court.

In 1975 it did not seem entirely far-fetched that the military would change its policy. After all, private industry had begun to adopt new hiring policies. Corporate giants such as AT&T, Bank of America, and IBM had banned employment discrimination based on sexual orientation. In July 1975, the federal Civil Service Commission quietly ended its policy against employing gay people.

But the military was unbending. Despite Matlovich's impeccable record, the air force, saying that he was unfit for service, recommended that he be given a general discharge (less than honorable but not dishonorable). Matlovich challenged the decision in federal court, vowing to take the case to the Supreme Court if necessary.

On May 26, 1975, Walter Cronkite, the highly respected anchor of the CBS Evening News, reported the case on television and aired an interview with Matlovich. Millions of viewers watched as Matlovich, a clean-cut, mannerly air force sergeant, explained why he could no longer hide his sexuality from the military: "My conscience wouldn't let me do it anymore," he said.

Matlovich later appeared on the cover of Time magazine, with the words "I Am a Homosexual" printed on the front. As the first openly gay person to challenge the military ban, he became one of the best-known gay men in the United States. Eventually, Matlovich agreed to a cash settlement from the air force. That is, he dropped his case against the military in exchange for payment. The ban against gays in the military remained in force. But Matlovich's story inspired other gay military personnel, male and female, to come forward with their own challenges.

■ ■ ■ ■ BACKLASH

As the 1970s progressed, gay rights activists chalked up further victories. Towns and cities across the country passed ordinances (laws) banning discrimination against gay people in hiring. By 1977 Craig Rodwell's old lover Harvey Milk was living in San Francisco and had become a gay activist. Milk was elected to the city's board of supervisors as an openly gay man. That same year, newly elected U.S. president Jimmy Carter and his adviser Midge Costanza invited a group of gay rights activists to the White House, the first such group to ever meet officially with a U.S. president. More gay characters appeared in television shows. David Kopay, a running back in the National Football League, came out of the closet.

Things seemed to be going so well that some gay rights activists worried the movement had become too relaxed. It had lost the urgency of the Stonewall years.

As gays and lesbians marched with more confidence into the

sunlight, though, many Americans glowered at them from behind pulled curtains. Some people were outraged that gays and lesbians were so visible, so forthright, and so demanding. In January 1977, this outrage found a voice. That month the city of Miami, Florida, passed an ordinance protecting gays from discrimination in housing, jobs, and other areas of public life. That meant, for instance, that a public school could not fire or refuse to hire someone simply for being gay.

Anita Bryant, a singer, former Miss America contestant, and spokesperson for Florida orange juice, adamantly opposed the ordinance. "The Bible says homosexuality is an abomination," she said. She vigorously objected to any law that would allow a gay person to teach her children.

Bryant launched an intense campaign against the ordinance. Her newly created organization, Save Our Children, collected more than one-half million signatures on a petition to force the ordinance to a vote by Dade County (Miami area) voters. The group's name, Save Our Children, played on all the old fears about gays and lesbians, as did Bryant's speeches. "Homosexuals cannot reproduce, so they must recruit," Bryant warned. The ordinance, she claimed, would unleash an onslaught of child pornography and turn Miami into a hotbed of uncontrolled gay lust.

Facing their first major challenge since Stonewall, gays rallied to fight the backlash. Supporters across the country contributed thousands of dollars to back the ordinance. But Anita Bryant and her supporters won big in Dade County. The ordinance was repealed. Soon similar ordinances were repealed in Wichita, Kansas; Saint Paul, Minnesota; and Eugene, Oregon. The tide seemed to be turning back against gay rights. Two weeks after the Dade County vote, Robert Hillsborough, a gay man, was violently murdered in San Francisco. A youth stabbed him fifteen times while repeatedly shouting, "Faggot!" Said Hillsborough's mother, "My son's blood is on her [Anita Bryant's] hands."

The battle lines were drawn. In California state senator John Briggs introduced Proposition 6, called the Briggs Initiative. It proposed banning gay teachers from the state's public schools. City supervisor Harvey Milk led the charge against the initiative. Milk liked a good fight. He would say, "Every movement needs something to push

Protesters gather outside San Francisco City Hall following the sentencing of Dan White in May 1979. White was found guilty of manslaughter, not murder, in the shooting deaths of Harvey Milk, gay rights activist and city supervisor, and Mayor George Moscone.

against," remembers Cleve Jones, a gay activist who was brought into the movement by Milk. In a debate over Proposition 6, Briggs said that gay teachers were "a greater danger than communism." But in November 1978, California voters soundly defeated the Briggs Initiative.

Less than a month later, Harvey Milk was dead. Dan White, his former colleague on the city's board of supervisors and an opponent of gay rights, had shot him to death at city hall. He also killed Mayor George Moscone, a gay rights supporter. That night forty thousand San Franciscans participated in a candlelight march to honor Milk.

The following May, a jury found Dan White guilty of manslaughter, not murder. (Murder is killing with malicious, or evil, intent. Manslaughter, a less serious crime, means killing without malice or premeditation.) Upon hearing the verdict, San Francisco's gay community stormed into the streets. In the "White Night" riots, gays and lesbians protested the verdict. They demonstrated against a society that said that murdering a gay man point-blank was merely manslaughter.

"Two days after I was elected, I got a phone call. The voice was quite young. It was from Altoona, Pennsylvania, and the person said, "Thanks." And you've got to elect gay people, so that that young child, and the thousands and thousands like that child, know that there's hope for a better world, there's hope for a better tomorrow. Without hope, not only gays, but those blacks, and the Asians, the disabled, the seniors, the us's, the us's, without hope, the us's give up. I know that you can't live on hope alone, but, without it, life is not worth living. [You] . . . have gotta give 'em hope."

TEN YEARS LATER

In 1979, if anyone needed proof that gays and lesbians had gained greater acceptance, they had only to look to Sioux City, South Dakota. Sioux City was hardly a hotbed of gay activism. Yet that spring, a young gay man named Randy Rohl brought his male date, Grady Quinn, to the high school prom. The event was not without tension. Someone had threatened Rohl, so the police were on hand. So was the media, in full force.

Rohl was uncomfortable with the attention. "Maybe it's a milestone in gay rights," he said, "but it's being made into more of a freak show." And why? "If you think about it," Rohl commented, "the sexual part of everyone's life is such a small part." Why use it to judge someone?

Another unmistakable sign of progress came on October 14, 1979, in Washington, D.C. That day the first National March on Washington for Lesbian and Gay Rights drew as many as 125,000 marchers. They came to the nation's capital to push for gay rights legislation.

The groups endorsing the march covered a range of gay-related interests. They included the National Coalition of Black Gays; the Lesbian Radio Collective of Detroit, Michigan; Lutherans Concerned for Gay People from Houston; the Gay Switchboard of Harrisburg, Pennsylvania; and Hispanic United Gays Liberado from New York. Not one of these groups had existed before the Stonewall riots.

Long-established organizations endorsed the march as well. These included the American Friends Service Committee, a Quaker organization, and labor organizations such as the AFL-CIO, the Actors' Equity Association, and the American Federation of Teachers. Their endorsements, too, were evidence of progress. It is unlikely they would have been willing to endorse such a march ten years earlier.

In the welcome message published in the march's program, Alan Young wrote, "We celebrate the 10th anniversary of the Stonewall Rebellion." He acknowledged the many people who had shepherded the gay rights movement to that moment in time.

Just after the Stonewall riots, young activists had been quick to

More than 125,000 people participated in the first National March on Washington for Lesbian and Gay Rights in October 1979.

In 1979, life partners Emery Hetrick and Damien Martin heard about a fifteen-year-old boy who had been gang-raped and then tossed out of a New York homeless shelter for being gay. They were moved to act. Hetrick, a psychiatrist, and Martin, a professor, created the Institute for the Protection of Lesbian and Gay Youth (later named the Hetrick-Martin Institute) in the city's East Village.

A year after opening, the institute had a caseload of 293 kids. Almost all had difficulties in school, where they faced harassment, physical abuse, and taunts for being gay. Institute staff realized that gay students needed a school where they felt safe. So in the mid-1980s, the institute founded Harvey Milk High School. The school is open to all students, though lesbian, gay, bisexual, and transgender youth make up most of the enrollment.

brush off old campaigners such as Barbara Gittings and Frank Kameny. But in 1979, Young acknowledged "the gay men and women of the pre-Stonewall era, who survived and especially those who spoke out against prejudice and ignorance." He named Gittings and Kameny and Bayard Rustin. Young even mentioned the Annual Reminder, which in the wake of Stonewall had struck some as unbelievably stodgy. Finally, the movement understood that those first steps by a small group of very brave people had laid the groundwork for all that followed.

Young wrote, "Today, in the capital of America, we are all here, the almost liberated and the slightly repressed . . . men in dresses and women in neckties; the nude and the prude, the beauties and the beasts. Yes, we are all here! We are everywhere! Welcome to the March on Washington for Gay and Lesbian Rights!"

CHAPTER 8

BECOMING INVINCIBLE

THE MODERN LGBTQ MOVEMENT

We don't have to ask for our rights; they're in the Constitution."

—activist Cleve Jones, August 30, 2009

In June 1981, the Centers for Disease Control and Prevention (CDC), a government health agency, reported that gay men in Los Angeles were getting a form of pneumonia that quickly led to death. About the same time, the *New York Times* reported that forty-one gay men had been diagnosed with a rare form of cancer, Kaposi's sarcoma. Eight of the men had died within months of the diagnosis. The pneumonia and the Kaposi's sarcoma turned out to be early signs of what became known as acquired immunodeficiency syndrome, or AIDS.

Medical researchers soon learned that AIDS was transmitted sexually and via infected blood. In 1984 scientists discovered the virus that causes AIDS—human immunodeficiency virus (HIV). By that time, more than one thousand gay men had died of the disease. In an article titled "1,112 and Counting," Larry Kramer warned gay men of the difficulty they were facing. "In all the history of homosexuality we have never before been so close to death and extinction," he wrote.

Yet many Americans seemed unconcerned about the deaths of so many gay men. The administration of President Ronald Reagan was notable for its silence on AIDS. Conservative minister Jerry Falwell even said that AIDS was a punishment from God for the "sin" of homosexuality. He failed to mention that gay men were not the only ones contracting the AIDS virus. Straight people were getting AIDS from sexual contact as well. People with AIDS also included IV drug users, people who had undergone blood transfusions with HIV-tainted blood, and babies born to women with HIV/AIDS. Around the world, more straight people than gay people contracted AIDS.

The AIDS crisis rallied the gay community. AIDS organizations raised public awareness of the disease, set up support networks for people with AIDS, and pressured lawmakers to increase funding for AIDS research. In addition, gay men and others tended to dying friends and lovers.

Cleve Jones wanted to commemorate victims of AIDS. In 1985 he envisioned creating a gigantic memorial quilt. Each block of the quilt, created by friends and family, would honor someone who had died of the disease. The quilt would tour the country.

In October 1987, the AIDS Memorial Quilt was displayed on the National Mall in Washington, D.C., as part of the second National March on Washington for Lesbian and Gay Rights.

In 1987 the AIDS Memorial Quilt, which included 1,920 panels, was displayed on the National Mall, in front of the U.S. Capitol, as part of the second National March on Washington for Lesbian and Gay Rights. "All the silence and fear and faith and love, every emotion of knowing and losing a loved one, was collected in one great memorial and laid out at the nation's door," Jones wrote.

BRANCHING OUT

Despite the enormous toll of the AIDS crisis, the gay rights movement made important advances in the 1980s. For one thing, families of gays and lesbians took a more active role in the movement. A support group called Parents, Families and Friends of Lesbians and Gays (PFLAG) formed in 1982.

Gay and lesbian youth, in particular, gained much-needed support in the 1980s. Nancy Garden, who in 1964 had picketed in front of the induction center on Whitehall Street, offered her support in the form of a book for young people. As a teenager, Garden had read Radclyffe Hall's *The Well of Loneliness*. The book has a sad ending. But "at the end there's an impassioned plea for justice and understanding," wrote Garden, "that made me vow to someday write a book about my people with a happy ending." In 1982 Garden published *Annie on My Mind*, a love story about teenage lesbians. True to her vow, Garden ended their story on a very encouraging note.

A volunteer talks to a caller on the PFLAG hotline in San Francisco, California, in September 1994. PFLAG offers help to lesbians and gays and their friends and families.

In Los Angeles, teacher Virginia Uribe learned of a young man named Chris who had dropped out of Fairfax High School after facing endless harassment for being gay. His own parents had kicked him out of the house when, at the age of fourteen, he told them he was gay. To help Chris and students like him, Uribe formed Project 10, which advocates for gay teens. In New York City in 1985, the Hetrick-Martin Institute opened Harvey Milk High School for gay and lesbian students. Many of its students had dropped out of other schools due to bullying.

THE NINETIES

The AIDS crisis wore on. Activists continued to push for increased government funding for AIDS research, prevention, and treatment. In the early 1990s, a leader in this fight was the AIDS Coalition to Unleash Power (ACT UP). Using the slogan "Silence = Death," ACT UP put the zap of the 1970s to work in the fight against AIDS. ACT UP targeted

U.S. senator Jesse Helms, who blamed AIDS on gay men's "disgusting, revolting conduct." In 1991, as a symbolic act of protest, ACT UP covered Helms's house in Arlington, Virginia, with a giant inflatable condom (condoms are one tool in AIDS prevention). ACT UP invited the media, which broadcast the story nationally.

By 1992 more than 150,000 Americans had died of AIDS. Hope seemed on the way in the form of Bill Clinton, the Democratic candidate for president. He courted the gay vote, acknowledging its political clout. Once elected, though, he failed to fully deliver for the gay movement.

For instance, Clinton had promised to repeal the ban on gays in the military. The idea created so much controversy that ultimately Clinton signed into law a policy known as Don't Ask, Don't Tell (DADT). Under this policy, the military would not ask about a person's sexual orientation. Gays and lesbians in the military would keep their sexual orientation to themselves. They would have to hide their identities to serve. If their sexuality were discovered or they tried to serve openly as gay, they would be discharged.

In 1996 Clinton signed into law the Defense of Marriage Act (DOMA). DOMA declares that the federal government defines marriage as a legal union strictly between a man and a woman. It says that even if certain states allow same-sex marriage, other states need not recognize those marriages. In 1996, however, no states did allow gay marriage. In fact, by then nearly every state had enacted statutes (laws) defining marriage as between a man and a woman.

> "I went downstairs to Dad's encyclopedia and looked up HOMOSEXUALITY, but that didn't tell me much about any of the things I felt. What struck me most, though, was that, in that whole long article, the word 'love' wasn't used even once."
>
> —Liza, in Annie on My Mind, *by Nancy Garden, 1982*

■ ■ ■ YOUNG AND GAY

The 1990s also saw an increase in gay activism among young people. They began to form gay-straight alliances (GSA) in their high schools, often despite opposition from some students and school administrators. In 1995, when the principal of East High School in Salt Lake City, Utah, refused to allow a group of students to form a GSA, the students successfully sued the school board.

Jamie Nabozny took on the system as an individual. Nabozny, a gay teenager in Ashland, Wisconsin, had endured bullying of the worst

Jamie Nabozny was bullied as a teenager in Wisconsin. He sued his former school district for failing to protect him from antigay bullies.

kind in middle and high school. Other students pretended to rape him and kicked him so viciously that he required surgery. Once two boys caught him alone in the school bathroom, shoved him into the urinal, and urinated on him. Nabozny and his parents reported the abuse to the school multiple times. But the school failed to adequately discipline the tormentors.

Nabozny attempted suicide a number of times, dropped out of school, and completed his high school education in another state. But he did not want to see other kids go through his nightmare. He sued his former school district for failing to protect him. In 1996 a court decided in his favor, awarding him a settlement of nine hundred thousand dollars. More important, the case established that schools must protect students from antigay harassment.

Nabozny became a gay activist and a speaker. Once in Texas, a young man came up to him after a speech. "When I was in high school," he

Gay college student Matthew Shepard was tortured and left to die by attackers in Wyoming in 1998.

told Nabozny, "I had the biggest picture of you on my locker. Every day the thing that got me through all of my classes was knowing that you were going to be there."

Abuse such as Nabozny suffered was rampant, but it rarely made mainstream news. Then, in October 1998, Matthew Shepard, a student at the University of Wyoming, was murdered because he was gay. His attackers tortured him and then tied him to a fence, leaving him to die in a remote area. When Shepard was found eighteen hours later, he was in a coma. He died soon after in the hospital. Shepard's story, which was widely reported, inspired new legislation to address antigay violence.

THE NEXT CENTURY

Forty years after the Stonewall riots, gays and lesbians are more visible and vocal and wield more political clout than ever before. The gay movement includes not only those attracted to people of their own gender but others whose gender identities and sexual orientation are outside of the heterosexual mainstream. The acronym LGBTQ, which stands for "lesbian, gay, bisexual, transgender, and questioning [of one's sexual orientation]," came into widespread use in the twenty-first century. The name reflects how the modern gay movement has expanded.

Every June, in commemoration of the June 1969 Stonewall riots, people across the United States and around the world hold Gay Pride parades and celebrations. At the same time, many gay and lesbian entertainers are open about their sexuality. They include Ellen

Thousands of people celebrate Gay Pride in San Francisco, California, on June 28, 2009.

DeGeneres, who not only hosts a popular TV show but also serves as a spokesmodel for CoverGirl cosmetics. *Brokeback Mountain*, a 2005 movie about the love between two cowboys, won three Academy Awards. A popular television show, *Degrassi: The Next Generation*, features teen gay and lesbian characters. In the workplace, 87 percent of Fortune 500 companies have policies that protect employees from discrimination based on sexual orientation. Fifty-one percent protect employees from discrimination based on gender identity.

It would seem that LGBTQs have been accepted into the mainstream. But one look at the day-to-day reality of being gay in the United States proves otherwise. For instance, most states do not permit gay people to adopt children. Only thirteen states and the District of Columbia ban discrimination based on sexual orientation or gender identity. In most states, hospitals can keep gay people from visiting their hospitalized partners, since only "immediate family," such as heterosexual spouses, are allowed to visit.

Don't Ask, Don't Tell remains in place in the U.S. military, although in September 2010, a federal judge ruled that the policy is unconstitutional. Also in September 2010, a federal district court ordered the U.S. Air Force to reinstate Major Margaret Witt, a flight nurse and a lesbian. After nineteen years in the service, Witt was discharged under Don't Ask, Don't Tell. The federal court held that the air force had failed to show that Witt's conduct had harmed her unit and thus ordered her reinstatement. Neither court ruling officially ends Don't Ask, Don't Tell, but both are important legal steps toward that goal.

GAY MARRIAGE

In 1999 the state of Vermont began allowing civil unions. These legal contracts granted same-sex couples some of the legal rights enjoyed by married heterosexual couples in Vermont. But partners in civil unions could not call their relationships marriages, nor did their legal rights extend across state lines. The first state to allow same-sex marriage was Massachusetts in 2004. Connecticut, Iowa, New Hampshire, and

WORTHY OF PRESERVATION

In 1999 the National Park Service nominated the Stonewall Inn for inclusion on the National Register of Historic Places. This is a list of historically important places in the United States that are worthy of preservation. Soon after the nomination was announced, antigay activists from a Kansas church protested in front of the inn. At the same time, a crowd of approximately one thousand counterprotesters gathered across the street. "We were able to drown them out," said counterprotester William Henderson, a veteran of the Stonewall riots. "Our numbers grew over the two-hour period while no one joined their side." The Stonewall Inn made it onto the National Register in 2000.

Vermont soon followed. In March 2010, the District of Columbia began allowing same-sex marriages. Frank Kameny was on hand to witness the district's first same-sex weddings.

The path to legalized same-sex marriage has been rocky in many jurisdictions. For instance, in the District of Columbia, opponents battled fiercely to defeat same-sex marriage legislation. California has been a major battleground in the marriage wars as well. In the spring of 2008, the California Supreme Court lifted a state ban on same-sex marriages, and gay couples flocked to the altar. But later that year, California voters passed Proposition 8, which again banned same-sex marriages. In August 2010, a federal judge in San Francisco struck down Proposition 8. The legal battle over same-sex marriage in California and other states is ongoing.

Because of the federal Defense of Marriage Act, even in states that allow same-sex marriages, gay couples do not enjoy equal rights with

A couple exchanges vows at San Francisco City Hall in 2008. Later that year, voters in California passed a law that banned same-sex marriages in the state.

To see where your state stands on gay marriage, visit the Lambda Legal website (www.lambalegal.org) or the National Gay and Lesbian Task Force website (www.thetaskforce.org). Both provide state-by-state information on laws involving gay marriage, employment discrimination, and gay adoption.

heterosexual couples. For instance, partners in gay marriages aren't entitled to the Social Security and Medicare benefits normally granted to married couples. Gay married couples can't file joint tax returns or take advantage of tax laws designed to help heterosexual married couples. The partners of gay military veterans aren't entitled to the benefits normally awarded to military spouses. The list goes on and on. In addition, the rights that gay married couples do enjoy in certain states don't travel with them when they cross into states that don't allow gay marriage.

MOVING AHEAD

Although many hurdles remain, the LGBTQ movement has evolved over the years in ways that bode well for its future success. The changes were evident at the October 2009 Equality March in Washington, D.C. The event drew more than two hundred thousand participants. The march, noted Urvashi Vaid, a longtime LGBTQ activist, "was called for by a grassroots younger generation," not the older, established organizations. "There is a new wave of activism coming up," she says. Out of the march came Equality Across America, a grassroots effort demanding equal rights, such as gay marriage and employment protection in all fifty states.

Activists cheer during the Equality March in Washington, D.C., on October 11, 2009. The event drew a new generation of LGBTQ activists.

The march was also noteworthy for the number of straight participants. In the beginning, gay marches primarily drew a gay crowd. However, American views have changed. In June 2010, according to a Gallup poll, for the first time, more than 50 percent of Americans said that they considered gay and lesbian relations morally acceptable. The most noteworthy findings involved the views of young people. In 2006, 42 percent of men between the ages of eighteen and forty-nine said they found gay and lesbian relations morally acceptable. By 2010 that number had jumped to 62 percent. For women in the same age group, the numbers went from 55 to 59 percent.

One of the most promising developments in the LGBTQ movement is the high level of youth activism. Constance McMillen, a high school student in Mississippi, took her high school to court when it refused to let her wear a tuxedo and bring a female date to the prom. In June 2010, McMillen appeared at the White House and lobbied Congress to pass the Student Non-Discrimination Act to ban discrimination based on sexual orientation in public schools.

Other schools have been far more supportive of their LGBTQ students. In Hudson, New York, in 2010 Charlie Ferrusi and Tim Howard, two gay best friends, wanted to run for prom king and queen at Hudson High School. First, they checked with their principal, who gave permission. Ferrusi and Howard's fellow students elected them in a landslide.

Thousands of GSAs have formed in high schools and colleges across the country. The Gay, Lesbian and Straight Education Network (GLSEN) works to ensure safe schools for all students. A group called Soulforce uses nonviolent protest, as practiced by Mohandas Gandhi, to increase understanding of LGBTQs. Each year it sponsors an Equality Ride. Its members travel by bus to conservative Christian colleges. There they talk with students about issues facing LGBTQ people.

Meanwhile, life as a gay or lesbian teen can still be tough. LGBTQ youth are four times more likely to attempt suicide than heterosexual youth, according to a 2006 survey. Those who are rejected by their families are nine times more likely to try suicide. Organizations such as the Trevor Project work to prevent suicide among LGBTQ youth. The Trevor Project telephone help line provides crisis and suicide prevention assistance around the clock. Dan Savage, a gay activist and commentator,

AN APOLOGY

In June 2009, the White House Office of Personnel Management (OPM) issued Frank Kameny an official apology for his 1957 dismissal from the Army Map Service. Calling it a "shameful action," OPM director John Berry wrote, "Please accept our apology for the consequences of the previous policy of the United States government." Berry, it should be noted, is gay.

"Apology accepted," responded Kameny.

also offers hope to troubled LGBTQ youth with his YouTube project "It Gets Better." In YouTube videos, gay, lesbian, and transgender adults tell how they survived bullying and became happy, successful adults.

FORTY YEARS LATER

On June 29, 2009, President Barack Obama hosted a celebration at the White House to mark the fortieth anniversary of the Stonewall riots. "Forty years ago, in the heart of New York City at a place called the Stonewall Inn," Obama said in his address, "a group of citizens, including a few who are here today... defied an unjust policy and awakened a nascent [new] movement." The president told the story of that night—how the Stonewall's customers did not disperse as usual following the raid: "On this night, something was different.... People didn't leave. They stood their ground. And over the course of several nights they declared that they had seen enough injustice in their time.... As we've seen so many times in history, once that spirit takes hold there is little that can stand in its way."

President Barack Obama *(top left)* speaks to a crowd at the White House on June 29, 2009. The reception marked the fortieth anniversary of the Stonewall riots.

Same-sex marriage is legal in the nations of Canada, Spain, the Netherlands, Belgium, Norway, Sweden, South Africa, and Argentina. In twenty-four nations, including Great Britain, Canada, Brazil, France, and Australia, gays and lesbians can serve openly in the military. However, in seventy-six countries, being gay is a crime. Seven nations punish homosexual acts by death.

The room was packed. Many of the guests were impatient with the president. Why was he dragging his feet on Don't Ask, Don't Tell? What about the Defense of Marriage Act? And yet they were there, in the White House, following in the footsteps of so many people who had come before them: Henry Gerber, Harry Hay, Barbara Gittings, Del Martin, Phyllis Lyon, the little band of protesters who had picketed the Whitehall Induction Center, and so many more. As for Frank Kameny, he was there in the flesh. What's more, the president addressing them, Barack Obama—the son of a white American mother and a black Kenyan father—was evidence that change was possible. In 1963, when Bayard Rustin had organized the March on Washington, it seemed far-fetched to think the United States would elect an African American president. Yet there was President Obama, standing on the shoulders of early civil rights activists.

In the 1950s and 1960s, gay and lesbian activists laid and lit the tinder for the LGBTQ movement. Then came the early morning hours of June 28, 1969. Craig Rodwell had shouted "Gay Power!" The tinder had burst into flame. The modern gay rights movement had begun. There would be no looking back.

1641: Puritans in Massachusetts adopt the Body of Laws, which says that homosexual acts are punishable by death.

1860s: Karl Maria Kertbeny first uses the term *homosexual* in pamphlets seeking repeal of the Prussian antihomosexuality laws.

1924: Henry Gerber founds the Society for Human Rights in Chicago to advocate for gay rights.

1929: Acting on a complaint by the New York Society for the Suppression of Vice, police seize eight hundred copies of Radclyffe Hall's book *The Well of Loneliness*, a lesbian love story.

1941: The U.S. military begins asking enlistees about their sexual orientation. Men and women who admit to homosexual tendencies are banned from serving.

1948: *Sexual Behavior in the Human Male* by Alfred C. Kinsey, better known as the Kinsey Report, becomes a best seller. Kinsey's findings indicate that 37 percent of males have engaged in some sort of homosexual sex.

1950: A comment by Deputy Secretary of State John Peurifoy sets off a witch hunt for homosexuals in the federal government and beyond.

1951: Donald Webster Cory (a pseudonym) publishes *The Homosexual in America*. Harry Hay and a small group of friends found the Mattachine Society in Los Angeles, dedicated to advancing the rights of the homosexual minority.

1952: The American Psychiatric Association publishes the first *Diagnostic and Statistical Manual of Mental Disorders*, which lists homosexuality as a sociopathic personality disturbance. George Jorgensen, a former soldier, undergoes sex reassignment surgery in Denmark and becomes Christine Jorgensen.

1953: President Dwight D. Eisenhower signs Executive Order 10450, which says that a government employee can be fired for "sexual perversion," that is, homosexuality.

1955: In San Francisco, Del Martin and Phyllis Lyon found the Daughters of Bilitis, a social group for lesbians.

1958: Barbara Gittings starts the New York City chapter of Daughters of Bilitis. The U.S. Supreme Court says that the homosexual publication ONE is not obscene and can legally be mailed through the U.S. Postal Service.

1961: Frank Kameny and Jack Nichols found a Mattachine Society chapter in Washington, D.C.

1964: A small group of gay men and women picket the Whitehall Induction Center in New York City to protest the ban on homosexuals in the military. The Society for Individual Rights (SIR) is founded in San Francisco.

1965: Police raid a fundraising ball for the Council on Religion and the Homosexual at California Hall in San Francisco. Mattachine of Washington, D.C., launches a series of pickets for homosexual rights. In *Scott v. Macy*, the U.S. Court of Appeals decides in favor of homosexual plaintiff Bruce Scott in a federal employment discrimination case.

1966: Drag queens riot at Gene Compton's Cafeteria in San Francisco.

1967: Craig Rodwell opens the Oscar Wilde Memorial Bookshop in New York City, the first gay bookstore in the United States.

1968: Frank Kameny coins the slogan "Gay Is Good." In California, Troy Perry holds the first service for gays and lesbians in what becomes the Metropolitan Community Church.

1969: Crowds of gay men, lesbians, and transgenders riot to protest a police raid at the Stonewall Inn in New York City's Greenwich Village. The Gay Liberation Front brings a new radical agenda to the gay rights movement. A group of gay men and lesbians found the Gay Activists Alliance, a militant group focusing solely on gay rights.

1970: The first Christopher Street Liberation Day march takes place in New York City on the anniversary of the Stonewall riots. Los Angeles groups sponsor a gay liberation parade.

1973: The American Psychiatric Association removes homosexuality from its list of mental illnesses.

1975: The federal government ends its policy of banning employment of gays and lesbians.

1977: Anita Bryant and her Save the Children organization successfully campaign to repeal a gay anti-discrimination ordinance in Miami, Florida.

1978: California voters reject the Briggs amendment, which would ban gay men and lesbians from teaching in the state's public schools. In San Francisco, Dan White assassinates gay city supervisor Harvey Milk and Mayor George Moscone.

1979: The first National March on Washington for Lesbian and Gay Rights draws more than 125,000 participants.

1981: Doctors diagnose the first AIDS cases.

1984: Researchers identify HIV, the virus that causes AIDS.

1987: The second National March on Washington for Lesbian and Gay Rights draws approximately a half million people to the nation's capital. The march marks the first public viewing of the AIDS Memorial Quilt.

1993: President Bill Clinton signs the Don't Ask, Don't Tell policy into law. Under DADT, gays and lesbians can serve in the military only if they hide their sexual orientation. The second National March on Washington for Lesbian and Gay Rights takes place.

1995: President Bill Clinton appoints the first White House liaison (representative) to the gay community.

1996: Congress passes the Defense of Marriage Act (DOMA), which defines marriage as a legal union between a man and a woman only. In *Romer v. Evans*, the U.S. Supreme Court strikes down an amendment to the Colorado state constitution that would bar gays and lesbians from challenging discrimination based on their sexual orientation.

1998: In Wyoming two men torture and murder Matthew Shepard for being gay.

2004: Massachusetts becomes the first state to legalize same-sex marriage.

2009: President Barack Obama recognizes the fortieth anniversary of the Stonewall riots with a reception at the White House.

2010: A federal judge overturns Proposition 8, which bans gay marriage in California. A federal judge rules that Don't Ask, Don't Tell is unconstitutional. A federal court orders the air force to reinstate Major Margaret Witt, who was discharged under Don't Ask, Don't Tell.

Henry Gerber

(1895–1972) Known as the "Grandfather of the American Gay Movement," Gerber was born in Bavaria and immigrated to the United States as a young man. In the early 1920s, he served in the U.S. military in Germany, where he was inspired by the country's dynamic gay culture and activism. Upon returning home to Chicago, he founded the Society for Human Rights to advocate for and protect the rights of homosexuals and anyone suffering abuse for being different. In 1925 police raided Gerber's home and arrested him for deviancy. Gerber later rejoined the army, and wrote articles for gay rights publications under a pseudonym. He died in 1972 in Washington, D.C.

Barbara Gittings

(1932–2007) Gittings, the child of a U.S. diplomat, was born in Austria. When she was a child, her family moved frequently before settling in Wilmington, Delaware. In 1956 she attended a meeting of the Daughters of Bilitis (DOB) in San Francisco, and in 1958, she founded the organization's New York City chapter. As editor of the DOB publication *The Ladder*, she pushed for the group to take a more activist stance. She participated in some of the earliest pickets for gay rights and worked closely with Frank Kameny to end the American Psychiatric Association's classification of homosexuality as a mental illness. She also worked with Kameny to challenge cases in which government employees had lost their security clearances due to homosexuality. In the post-Stonewall era, she became involved in the American Library Association, advocating for books by and about gay people and establishing the ALA's annual Gay Book Award.

Harry Hay

(1912–2002) Hay, who was born in Britain, moved to Los Angeles with his family as a boy. Dismayed by the economic ruin of the Great Depression, Hay joined the Communist Party in the 1930s. Although he knew he was a homosexual, he married Anita Platky, a fellow Communist Party member. They later divorced. On November 11, 1951, in Los Angeles, Hay and four friends held the first meeting of the Mattachine Society, a secret organization for promoting and protecting the rights of the homosexual minority. Hay's background as a Communist was so troubling to new members that Hay chose to resign rather than inhibit Mattachine's growth. In his later years, he studied Native American culture, advocated for marginalized members of the gay movement such as drag queens, and established the Radical Faeries, a group that advocates political activism while nurturing gay spirituality.

Franklin Kameny

(1925–) Kameny, born in Queens, New York, decided at six years old that he wanted to be an astronomer. During World War II, he served as a U.S. Army mortar crewman. After the war, he earned a scholarship to Harvard and graduated with a Ph.D. in astronomy. In the 1950s, he worked for the federal government's Army Map Service. In 1957 the government dismissed him after learning that he was homosexual. Kameny fought his dismissal, first through administrative channels and then through the federal courts. In 1961 Kameny and Jack Nichols founded the Mattachine Society of Washington (MSW). MSW challenged a range antigay practices, including government dismissals, the military ban on homosexuals, and police raids on gay bars. Kameny coined the slogan "Gay Is Good" in 1968. He played a major role in the American Psychiatric Association decision to remove homosexuality from its list of mental illnesses and the federal government's 1975 decision to end the ban on homosexual employees.

Phyllis Lyon and Del Martin

(1924– and 1921–2008) Lyon was born in Tulsa, Oklahoma, but spent much of her childhood in the San Francisco area. She majored in journalism at the University of California at Berkeley. Martin grew up in San Francisco and also attended the University of California at Berkeley as a journalism major. Lyon and Martin met and fell in love when they were both working in Seattle. They moved to San Francisco in 1953. In 1955 they formed the Daughters of Bilitis (DOB), the first lesbian organization in the United States. Lyon became the first editor of *The Ladder*, the DOB publication, and Martin became the second editor. In 1964 they began working with Ted McIlvenna and the Council on Religion and the Homosexual. Lyon eventually became the administrative assistant for CRH. Lyon and Martin became active in the National Organization for Women (NOW) in the early 1970s and advocated for lesbian concerns within the organization. In 2004 they were the first same-sex couple in California to apply for a marriage license, and in 2008, when the state first legalized same-sex marriage, they became the first same-sex couple to marry.

Harvey Milk

(1930–1978) Harvey Milk was born in Woodmere, New York, near New York City. As a teenager, he realized he was gay, but he kept his sexuality a secret. Milk earned his bachelor's degree from the New York State College for Teachers in 1951. He then joined the U.S. Navy. He served as an officer on a submarine during the Korean War. After leaving the navy in 1955, Milk began teaching at a New York City high school. In the early 1960s, he switched careers, taking a job with an investment firm. As the 1960s progressed, Milk became more politically active. He lived openly as a gay man and protested against the Vietnam War. In 1972 he moved to San Francisco with his romantic partner. The two men opened a camera shop on Castro Street, the center of the city's gay community. Milk became active in politics. He organized the San Francisco Gay Democratic Club and ran for the city's Board of Supervisors. He lost two elections before finally winning a seat on the board in 1977. As a supervisor, Milk spearheaded the passage of several gay rights laws. He also worked on behalf of minorities, poor people, and the elderly. Another city supervisor, Dan White, opposed Milk's work on gay rights. White killed both Milk and San Francisco mayor George Moscone in 1978. In the years since his death, Harvey Milk's status as a gay rights hero has soared. Schools, clubs, and parades are named in his honor. He was the subject of an award-winning documentary film in 1984. In 2008 acclaimed actor Sean Penn played Milk in a major Hollywood movie, Milk.

Craig Rodwell

(1940–1993) Rodwell grew up mostly in Chicago. He moved to New York City in the late 1950s. He volunteered at the Mattachine office and took over most of the work of producing the organization's newsletter. He also had a romantic relationship with Harvey Milk, who at that time was closeted. In 1964 Rodwell participated in the first picket for homosexual rights in front of New York City's Whitehall Induction Center. In 1965 he participated in the Mattachine Society of Washington's picket in front of the White House. He came up with the Annual Reminder, an annual picket on the Fourth of July in front of Philadelphia's Independence Hall. In 1967 he opened the Oscar Wilde Memorial Bookshop in Greenwich Village, the first gay bookstore in the United States. On the first night of the Stonewall riots, he galvanized the crowd with his cries for "Gay Power!" Soon after the riots, he came up with the idea to commemorate the one-year anniversary of the riots with the Christopher Street Liberation Day march. The march evolved into Gay Pride Week.

bisexual: a person who is attracted, sexually and emotionally, to both males and females

drag queen: a man who dresses up as a woman, complete with makeup, women's shoes, and a wig

entrapment: the act of luring someone into committing a crime in order to arrest him or her. In the past, undercover policemen lured gay men into agreeing to have sex and then arrested them.

gay: a slang term for a person who is attracted, sexually and emotionally, to persons of the same sex. While *gay* can refer to all genders, it can also mean just gay men.

heterosexual: a person who is attracted, sexually and emotionally, to persons of the opposite gender. The slang term is *straight*.

homosexual: a person who is attracted, sexually and emotionally, to persons of his or her own gender

lesbian: a woman who is primarily attracted, sexually and emotionally, to other women. The term derives from the island of Lesbos, home to Sappho, an ancient Greek poet and lesbian.

LGBTQ: an acronym for lesbian, gay, bisexual, transgender, and questioning. Questioning refers to people who are unsure of their sexual orientation.

straight: heterosexual

transgender: a broad term for anyone whose gender identity does not correspond to his or her gender at birth—for instance, a man who prefers to wear women's clothing

transsexual: a person whose gender identity is the opposite of his or her biological sex at birth. Transsexuals sometimes undergo gender transition surgery.

5 Patrick Grace, interview with editor, October 14, 2010.

5 David Carter, *Stonewall: The Riots That Sparked the Gay Revolution* (New York: St. Martin's Press, 2004), 147.

6 Walt Whitman, "Leaves of Grass (1891–92)," Walt Whitman Archive, 1995–2010, http://www.whitmanarchive.org/published/LG/1891/poems/190 (October 14, 2010).

7 Home Box Office, *The Sopranos*, season 4, episode 12, "Eloise," 2002.

7 Larry Kramer, "Homo Sex in Colonial America," *Huffington Post*, May 19, 2009, http://www.huffingtonpost.com/larry-kramer/homo-sex-in-colonial-amer_b_205399.html (August 20, 2010).

8 *New York Times*, "A Most Shocking Crime," January 26, 1892, 1.

9 *New York Times*, "Jealousy the Motive," January 29, 1892, 1.

9 *Washington Post*, "The Opinion of an Expert," July 24, 1892, 1.

9 *Washington Post*, "Eloped with Her Girl Friend," March 18, 1892, 4.

9 Hanover Historical Texts Project, "The Massachusetts Body of Liberties," 1641, Hanover Historical Texts Project, August 1996, http://history.hanover.edu/texts/masslib.htm (August 20, 2010).

9–10 Ibid.

10 Louis Crompton, "Homosexuals and the Death Penalty in Colonial America," University of Nebraska-Lincoln, 1976, http://digitalcommons.unl.edu/cgi/viewcontent.cgi?article=1061&context=englishfacpubs (August 20, 2010).

10 Ibid.

10 Ibid.

11 Ibid.

12 Havelock Ellis, "Studies in the Psychology of Sex," Project Gutenberg, 2004, http://www.gutenberg.org/files/13611/13611-h/13611-h.htm (August 20, 2010).

12 Ibid.

12 Ibid.

14 Kramer, "Homo Sex in Colonial America."

14 Ibid.

15 J. Brooks Atkinson, "The Play," *New York Times*, September 30, 1926, 23.

16 Malinda Lo, "Back in the Day: Emerging from the Well of Loneliness," After Ellen.com, July 2005, http://www.afterellen.com/archive/ellen/column/2005/7/backintheday.html (August 20, 2010).

17 David Smith, "Lesbian Novel Was 'Danger to Nation,'" *Guardian* (London), January 2, 2005, http://www.guardian.co.uk/uk/2005/jan/02/books.gayrights (October 14, 2010).

17 Diane Souhami, *Trials of Radclyffe Hall* (New York: Doubleday, 1999), 234.

17 Ibid., 235.

17 Ibid., 216.

18 John D'Emilio, *Lost Prophet: The Life and Times of Bayard Rustin* (New York: Free Press, 2003), 16.

18 Devon W. Carbado and Donald Weise, eds., *Time on Two Crosses: The Collected Writings of Bayard Rustin* (San Francisco: Cleis Press, 2003), 283.

20 Allan Bérubé, *Coming Out Under Fire: The History of Gay Men and Women in World War II* (New York: Penguin Books, 1991), 212.

21 Casey Adair and Nancy Adair, *Word Is Out: Stories of Some of Our Lives,* (New York: Dell, 1978), 56.

21 Ibid., 57.

22 Bérubé, *Coming Out Under Fire*, 8.

23 Ibid., 114.

23 Ibid., 196.

24 Ibid., 226.

24 Ibid., 180.

24 Ibid., 221.

24–25 Ibid., 222.

26 Ibid., 212.

27 Adair and Adair, *Word Is Out*, 61.

28 Randy Shilts, *Conduct Unbecoming: Gays and Lesbians in the U.S. Military* (New York: St. Martin's Press, 2005), 107–108.

29 *Time*, "Manners & Morals: How to Stop Gin Rummy," March 1, 1948, http://www.time.com/time/magazine/article/0,9171,794270,00.html (August 1, 2010).

30 Gore Vidal, "The City and the Pillar," *Threepenny Review*, Summer 1995, http://www.threepennyreview.com/samples/vidal_su95.html (August 10, 2010).

30 *Washington Post*, "The City and the Pillar," January 11, 1948, B7.

31 Charles Kaiser, *The Gay Metropolis: The Landmark History of Gay Life in America since World War II* (San Diego: Harcourt, Brace and Company, 1997), 56.

32 John D'Emilio, *Sexual Politics, Sexual Communities: The Making of a Homosexual Minority in the United States, 1940–1970* (Chicago: University of Chicago Press, 1983), 125.

34 David Halberstam, *The Fifties* (New York: Villard Press, 1993), 50.

34 William S. White, "Never Condoned Disloyalty, Says Acheson of His Stand," *Washington Post*, March 1, 1950, 1.

34 Edward F. Ryan, "Senate Unit Sharply Divided on Federal Pervert Problem," *Washington Post*, March 28, 1950, 1.

35 Jerry Kluttz, "Names of 200 Perverts Listed for Firing by U.S. Agencies," *Washington Post*, May 9, 1950, 1.

35 Kaiser, *Gay Metropolis*, 69.

38 Adair and Adair, *Word Is Out*, 5, 7.

39 D'Emilio, *Sexual Politics*, 62.

39 Ibid., 68.

42 Ibid., 69.

42 Ibid., 71.

42 Marcia Gallo, *Different Daughters: A History of the Daughters of Bilitis and the Rise of the Lesbian Rights Movement* (Carrrol & Graf Publishers, 2006), 2.

43 D'Emilio, *Sexual Politics*, 125.

45 Vern L. Bullough, *Before Stonewall: Activists for Gay and Lesbian Rights in Historical Context* (New York: Harrington Park Press, 2002), 211.

45 Kaiser, *Gay Metropolis*, 138–39.

46 Ibid., 106.

47 *Time*, "The Press: The Great Transformation," December 15, 1952, http://www.time.com/time/magazine/article/0,9171,820503,00.html (August 20, 2010).

47 *Washington Post*, "Parents Join Ex-GI, Now a Daughter," December 21, 1952, M3.

48 Frank Fitch, "Remember California Hall," *Vector*, February 1973, available online at LGBT Religious Achives Network, n.d., http://www.lgbtran.org/Exhibits/CRH/Room.aspx?RID=6&CID=29 (August 20, 2010).

50 Ibid.

50 Bullough, *Before Stonewall*, 275.

52 Kameny Papers, "Correspondence," Kameny Papers, June 10, 2010, http://www.kamenypapers.org/correspondence.htm (August 20, 2010).

52 Bullough, *Before Stonewall*, 242.

52 Carter, *Stonewall*, 36.

54 D'Emilio, *Lost Prophet*, 338.

54–55 Ibid., 339.

55 Carbado and Weise, *Time on Two Crosses*, 286.

55 D'Emilio, *Lost Prophet*, 347.

56 Nancy Garden, e-mail to author, April 12, 2010.

56 Ibid.

56–57 Ibid.

57 Ibid.

57 Jack Nichols, "The Gay Civil Rights Movement Turns to Public Picketing, Rainbow History Project, 2010, http://www.rainbowhistory.org/Pickets.htm (August 20, 2010).

57 Ibid.

57 Martin Duberman, *Stonewall* (New York: Dutton, 1993), 113.

59 Susan Stryker, *Transgender History* (Berkeley, CA: Seal Press, 2008), 65.

62 Garden, e-mail.

63 Webster Scott, "Civil Rights and the Homosexual," *New York Times*, November 12, 1967, 271.

63 *Boys in the Band*, display ad, *New York Times*, April 17, 1968, 41.

64 Carter, *Stonewall*, 147.

66 Ibid.

67 Yvonne Ritter, Tommy Lanigan-Schmidt, Danny Garvin, and David Carter, "Stonewall Rebellion Discussion," LGBTQ Civil Rights Movement, June 2, 2008, http://www.housing.wisc.edu/diversity/lgbtclass/stonewell.php (August 20, 2010).

68 Carter, *Stonewall*, 137.

68 Ibid, 138.

68 Ibid., 139.

69 Ibid., 141.

70 Ibid., 147.

70 Jeffrey Slonim, "Talking Stonewall," *Interview*, June 1994.

70 Carter, *Stonewall*, 149.

70 Ibid.

70 Ibid., 150.

72 David Eisenbach, *Gay Power: An American Revolution* (New York: Carroll and Graf, 2006), 93.

72 Carter, *Stonewall*, 167.

72 Ibid., 172.

73 Ibid., 175.

73 Ibid., 175–76.

73 Ritter, Lanigan-Schmidt,

Garvin, and Carter, "Stonewall Rebellion Discussion."

74 Ibid., 178.

74 Duberman, Stonewall, 201.

74 Carter, Stonewall, 178.

75 Ibid., 162.

75 Ibid., 185.

76 Ibid. 196.

76 Ibid., 195.

77 Ibid., 196.

77 Ibid., 210.

78 Ibid., 202.

78–79 Ibid.

79 Thomas Duane, "From Stonewall to the Capitol," Advocate, June 22, 1999, 11.

79 Carter, Stonewall, 202.

79 Ibid., 204.

80 Neil Miller, Out of the Past: Gay and Lesbian History from 1869 to the Present (New York: Vintage Books, 1995), 385.

81 Duberman, Stonewall, 210.

82 Carter, Stonewall, 215–216.

82 Eisenbach, Gay Power, 140.

82 Ibid., 136.

84 Carter, Stonewall, 224.

85 Ibid., 241.

86 Ibid.

87 Ibid., 244.

87 Grace Glueck, "For Museum Birthday, Good Cheer and Cake," New York Times, April 14, 1970, 1.

87 Carter, Stonewall, 244.

88 New York Times, display ad, April 17, 1970, 41.

88 Clive Barnes, "Stage: Birthday for 'Boys in the Band," New York Times, April 18, 1970, 34.

88 Eisenbach, Gay Power, 138.

90 Duberman, Stonewall, 272.

91 Ibid., 278.

91 Eisenbach, Gay Power, 110.

92 Duberman, Stonewall, 279.

92 Carter, Stonewall, 254.

92 Dudley Clendinen and Adam Nagourney, Out for Good: The Struggle to Build a Gay Rights Movement in America (New York: Simon and Schuster, 1999), 64.

92 New Yorker, "Talk of the Town: Parade," July 11, 1970, 20.

93 Troy Perry, "Troy Perry's Pride: June, 1970 Saw the Nation's First Gay Pride Parades," Advocate, June 19, 2007, http://www.highbeam.com/doc/1G1-164719415.html (August 20, 2010).

93 Ibid.

94 Harvey Milk, "The Hope Speech," excerpt available online at Haunt of Victory, August 2010, http://victormv.wordpress.com/2008/09/08/harvey-milk-the-hope-speech-excerpt (August 20, 2010).

95 Elaine Noble, "Elaine Noble," Out History, 2009, http://www.outhistory.org/wiki/Elaine_Noble (August 20, 2010).

96 Clendinen and Nagourney, Out for Good, 201.

96 Ibid., 202.

97 Ibid., 204.

97 Ibid., 206.

97–98 Ibid., 216.

99 Miller, Out of the Past, 411.

100 "Gay Pioneer Leonard Matlovich First TV Interview," YouTube, 2010, http://www.youtube.com/watch?v=kUIt_ZUfkqE (August 20, 2010).

101 Time, "Gay Rights Showdown in Miami," June 13, 1977, http://www.time.com/time/magazine/article/0,9171,918998,00.html (September 27, 2010).

101 Miller, *Out of the Past*, 402.

101 Ibid., 403.

101–102 Cleve Jones, *Stitching a Revolution: The Making of an Activist*, with Jeff Dawson (New York: HarperCollins, 2000) 39.

102 Ibid., 51.

103 "Harvey Milk Speech," YouTube, November 11, 2008, http://www.youtube.com/watch?v=MbWDNM0wuAc (August 20, 2010).

103 Karren Mills, Associated Press, "Gay Pride Pioneer's Life Included Friendships, Dreams and Death," *Los Angeles Times*, February 27, 1994, http://articles.latimes.com/1994-02-27/news/mn-27881_1_lincoln-high-school (August 20, 2010).

104 Alan Young, "Welcome to the March," National March on Washington for Lesbian and Gay Rights, 1979, http://www.rainbowhistory.org/mowprogram.pdf (August 20, 2010).

105 Ibid.

105 Ibid.

106 Bill Browning, "Cleve Jones: The Man Behind the Curtain," Bilerico Project, September 1, 2009, http://www.bilerico.com/2009/09/cleve_jones_the_man_behind_the_curtain.php (August 20, 2010).

107 Clendinen and Nagourney, *Out for Good*, 480.

109 Carbado and Weise, *Time on Two Crosses*, 278.

109 Clendinen and Nagourney, *Out for Good*, xviii.

109 Nancy Garden, *Annie on My Mind* (New York: Farrar, Straus and Giroux, 2007), 243.

111 Peter Staley, "In Memory of Jesse Helms and the Condom I Put on His House," Poz Blogs, July 8, 2008, http://blogs.poz.com/peter/archives/2008/07/in_memory_of_je.html (August 20, 2010).

111 Garden, *Annie on My Mind*, 143.

112–113 *People Weekly*, "Growing Up Gay," August 17, 1998, 44.

115 Clemente Lisi, "Anti-gay Protesters Run into Stonewall," *New York Post*, September 12, 1999, http://www.stonewallvets.org/ (August 20, 2010).

117 Urvashi Vaid, "The Fight for Equality: A Look at the State of the Gay Rights Movement," interviewed by Sharif Abdel Kouddous and Amy Goodman, transcript *Democracy Now!*, October 13, 2009, http://www.democracynow.org/2009/10/13/the_fight_for_equality_a_look (August 20, 2010).

119 "Gay Rights Activist Frank Kameny Gets Apology from U.S. Govt.," Towleroad, June 25, 2009, http://www.towleroad.com/2009/06/gay-rights-activist-frank-kameny-gets-apology-from-us-govt.html (August 20, 2010).

120 "Obama White House LGBT Stonewall Fete: Transcript, Guest List, Video," Towleroad, June 29, 2009, http://www.towleroad.com/2009/06/obamas-white-house-lgbt-stonewall-event-transcript-guest-list.html (August 20, 2010).

SELECTED BIBLIOGRAPHY

Adair, Casey, and Nancy Adair. *Word Is Out: Stories of Some of Our Lives*. New York: Dell, 1978.

Bérubé, Allan. *Coming Out Under Fire: The History of Gay Men and Women in World War II*. New York: Penguin Books, 1991.

Bullough, Vern L. *Before Stonewall: Activists for Gay and Lesbian Rights in Historical Context*. New York: Harrington Park Press, 2002.

Carbado, Devon W., and Donald Weise, eds. *Time on Two Crosses: The Collected Writings of Bayard Rustin*. San Francisco: Cleis Press, 2003.

Carter, David. *Stonewall: The Riots That Sparked the Gay Revolution*. New York: St. Martin's Press, 2004.

Clendinen, Dudley, and Adam Nagourney. *Out for Good: The Struggle to Build a Gay Rights Movement in America*. New York: Simon and Schuster, 1999.

D'Emilio, John. *Lost Prophet: The Life and Times of Bayard Rustin*. New York: Free Press, 2003.

———. *Sexual Politics, Sexual Communities: The Making of a Homosexual Minority in the United States, 1940–1970*. Chicago: University of Chicago Press, 1983.

Duberman, Martin. *Stonewall*. New York: Dutton, 1993.

Eisenbach, David. *Gay Power: An American Revolution*. New York: Carroll and Graf, 2006.

Faderman, Lillian, and Stuart Timmons. *Gay L.A.: A History of Sexual Outlaws, Power Politics, and Lipstick Lesbians*. New York: Basic Books, 2006.

Garden, Nancy. *Hear Us Out! Lesbian and Gay Stories of Struggle, Progress, and Hope, 1950 to the Present*. New York: Farrar, Straus and Giroux, 2007.

Jay, Karla. *Tales of the Lavender Menace: A Memoir of Liberation*. New York: Basic Books, 2000.

Jones, Cleve. *Stitching a Revolution: The Making of an Activist*. With Jeff Dawson. New York: HarperCollins, 2000.

Kaiser, Charles. *The Gay Metropolis: The Landmark History of Gay Life in America since World War II*. San Diego: Harcourt, Brace and Company, 1997.

Miller, Neil. *Out of the Past: Gay and Lesbian History from 1869 to the Present*. New York: Vintage Books, 1995.

Sears, James T. *Lonely Hunters: An Oral History of Lesbian and Gay Southern Life, 1948–1968*. Boulder, CO: Westview Press, 1997.

Shilts, Randy. *Conduct Unbecoming: Gays and Lesbians in the U.S. Military*. New York: St. Martin's Press, 2005.

Stryker, Susan. *Transgender History*. Berkeley, CA: Seal Press, 2008.

Vaid, Urvashi. *Virtual Equality: The Mainstreaming of Gay and Lesbian Liberation*. New York: Anchor, 1995.

Books

Alsenas, Linas. *Gay America*. New York: Amulet Books, 2008. Alsenas presents a history of gays and lesbians in the United States from the Victorian era through the present. Engaging individual stories introduce readers to the broader history of each era.

Andryszewski, Tricia. *Same-Sex Marriage: Moral Wrong or Civil Right?* Minneapolis: Twenty-First Century Books, 2008. This book for high schoolers explores the topic of same-sex marriage and civil unions in a balanced, thought-provoking way that encourages critical thinking about the issue.

Bauer, Marion Dane, ed. *Am I Blue? Coming Out from the Silence*. New York: HarperCollins, 1994. Popular young adult and children's authors wrote the eighteen stories in this anthology, which introduce young gay teens and lesbian characters facing first love, coming out, and other experiences.

Cart, Michael, ed. *How Beautiful the Ordinary: Twelve Stories of Identity*. New York: HarperCollins, 2009. The twelve stories in this anthology, all written by acclaimed young adult authors, offer insights into the lives of gay, lesbian, and transgender youth.

Garden, Nancy. *Annie on My Mind*. New York: Farrar, Straus and Giroux, 2007. Nancy Garden's groundbreaking book is a love story about two teenage lesbians. Annie and Liza learn to come to terms with their sexuality while dealing with the ups and downs of their first romantic relationship.

Heron, Ann. *Two Teenagers in 20: Writings by Gay and Lesbian Youth*. New York: Alyson Publications, 1995. The forty-plus autobiographical narratives by gay and lesbian teens that comprise this collection address homophobia, family rejection, meeting other gay people, and more.

Images and Issues series. Minneapolis: Twenty-First Century Books, 2008. This series by Catherine Gourley discusses the social and political representations of women through American history. *Gidgets and Women Warriors: Perceptions of Women in the 1950s and 1960s* examines changing views of women—from the conformist 1950s through the rebellious 1960s. *Ms. and the Material Girls: Perceptions of Women from the 1970s through the 1990s* highlights the changes for women in those decades. Gourley looks at advertisements, popular magazines, and other media to explore how women of this time were perceived and how they perceived themselves.

Jennings, Kevin. *Becoming Visible: A Reader in Gay and Lesbian History for High School and College Students*. Boston: Alyson, 1994. This book offers readings about gay and lesbian history from around the world, going back to the ancient Greeks and ending in the present day.

Levithan, David, and Billy Merrell. *The Full Spectrum: A New Generation of Writing about Gay, Lesbian, Bisexual, Transgender, Questioning, and Other Identities.* New York: Alfred A. Knopf, 2006. Essays, poems, and photographs, all by people under the age of twenty-three, offer insights into being gay, lesbian, bisexual, transgender, and questioning.

Summer, Jane. *Not the Only One: Lesbian and Gay Fiction for Teens.* New York: Alyson Books, 2004. The twenty stories about young gays and lesbians in this anthology deal with coming out, gay-bashing, falling in love, and more.

Films

Stonewall Uprising. DVD. Directed by Kate Davis and David Heilbroner. New York City: First Run Features, 2010. Stonewall patrons, reporters, and police recount the story of the Stonewall riots in this documentary. The film also examines what life was like for most homosexuals before the riots, when they were viewed as predatory perverts, faced rampant police entrapment, and endured drastic psychiatric treatments.

The Times of Harvey Milk. DVD. New York: New Yorker Video, 1984. This documentary follows gay political activist Harvey Milk from his closeted days in New York City to his embrace of gay liberation in San Francisco, where in 1977 he became the first openly gay man elected to the city's board of supervisors. The movie also examines Milk's murder by fellow city supervisor Dan White and the gay rights activism that followed.

Websites

Advocate
http://www.advocate.com
The *Advocate* is a leading LBGTQ news publication.

Gay, Lesbian and Straight Education Network (GLSEN)
http://www.glsen.org
This national organization works to ensure that all members of school communities are treated with respect, regardless of sexual orientation or gender identity.

GLBT History Month website
http://www.glbthistorymonth.com
This website celebrates Gay History Month in October by identifying the achievements of a different LGBTQ icon for each day of the month. The site includes video, biographies, images, educational resources, and more.

GSA/Gay Straight Alliance Network
  http://www.gsanetwork.org
  The GSA Network helps youth activists—LGBTQ and straight—form gay-straight
  alliance organizations, connect with other GSAs across the country, and provide
  resources and leadership.

Human Rights Campaign (HRC)
  http://www.hrc.org
  HRC is the nation's largest national LGBTQ civil rights organization.

Lambda Legal Defense
  http://www.lambdalegal.org
  Lambda is a national legal organization devoted to the cause of LGBTQ equality.
  The website offers an excellent state-by-state information guide on key LGBTQ
  legal issues.

LGBT Religious Archives Network
  http://www.lgbtran.org/
  The LGBT Religious Archives Network seeks to preserve and present the history
  of the LGBT religious movements around the world. The site includes a first-rate
  online exhibit about the Council on Religion and the Homosexual and the 1965
  raid on California Hall.

Matthew Shepard Foundation
  http://www.matthewshepard.org
  This foundation honors Matthew Shepard's legacy by working to fight hate and
  to build understanding for LGBTQ people. The website also offers an online
  community for LGBTQ youth and their allies at Matthew's Place (clickable from
  the home page).

New York Public Library
  1969: The Year of Gay Liberation Online Exhibit
  http://legacy.www.nypl.org/research/chss/1969/liberation.html
  This excellent online exhibit covers the events leading up to the Stonewall riot,
  the riot itself, and the immediate aftermath of the riots.

OutHistory Fight against Forgetting
  http://www.outhistory.org
  This website is dedicated to LGBTQ history. It includes a range of online
  exhibits, educational resources, and images.

Parents, Family and Friends of Lesbians and Gays (PFLAG)
  http://www.pflag.org
  PFLAG works to promote the health and well-being of LBGTQ persons and their
  families and friends via support, education, and advocacy work.

Rainbow History Project

http://www.rainbowhistory.org

The Rainbow History Project works to preserve LGBTQ history from the Washington, D.C., area. It includes online exhibits, oral histories, and other material from the Mattachine Society of Washington, including a link to Frank Kameny's milestone 1964 speech to New York Mattachine Society.

Stonewall Veterans' Association

http://www.Stonewallvets.org

The Stonewall Veterans' Association website offers a look at the Stonewall Inn and the riots from the viewpoint of those who were there in 1969. The website includes photographs, old newspaper articles, and the story behind naming the Stonewall a National Historic Landmark.

Trevor Project

http://www.thetrevorproject.org

The Trevor Project aims to promote acceptance of LGBTQ youth. It offers suicide prevention assistance and help to LGBTQ youth in crisis.

University of Madison: LGBT Civil Rights Movement

http://www.housing.wisc.edu/diversity/lgbtclass/index.php

This online exhibit/classroom documents a University of Wisconsin–Madison course, "The LGBTQ Civil Rights Movement—1960–1990." During the class, students visited historic LGBTQ sites and met with LGBTQ movement veterans. The website includes excellent oral history transcripts from Stonewall participants and other gay rights movement activists.

PHOTO ACKNOWLEDGMENTS

The images in this book are used with the permission of: Swarthmore College Peace Collection, p. 8; © North Wind Picture Archives, p. 10; © Mary Evans Picture Library/Sigmund Freud Copyrights/The Image Works, p. 12; © Edwin Levick/ Archive Photos/Getty Images, p. 15; © Russell/Hulton Archive/Getty Images, p. 16; © Charles E. Steinheimer/Time & Life Pictures/Getty Images, p. 21; © Roger Viollet/Getty Images, p. 22; Library of Congress, pp. 25 (LC-USW33-027849-ZC), 30 (LC-USZ62-121307); © Arthur Siegel/Time & Life Pictures/Getty Images, p. 29; AP Photo/Herbert White, p. 33; © Harry Hay, p. 39; © John Gruber, p. 40; Courtesy of Phyllis Lyon, p. 43; © Evening Standard/Hulton Archive/Getty Images, p. 46; AP Photo, pp. 47, 54, 57, 60-61, 102; © Fred W. McDarrah/Getty Images, pp. 51, 74, 77; Barbara Gittings and Kay Tobin Lahusen gay history papers and photographs, Manuscripts and Archives Division, The New York Public Library, Astor, Lenox and Tilden Foundations, pp. 53, 62, 86; Diana Davies photographs, Manuscripts and Archives Division, The New York Public Library, Astor, Lenox and Tilden Foundations, pp. 65, 89; © New York Daily News Archive via Getty Images, p. 71; © Larry Morris/ The New York Times/Redux, p. 78; © Laura Westlund/Independent Picture Service, p. 83; © Ellen Shumsky/The Image Works, p. 84; © JP Laffont/Sygma/CORBIS, p. 91; © Grey Villet/Time & Life Pictures/Getty Images, p. 93; Manuscripts and Archives Division, The New York Public Library, Astor, Lenox and Tilden Foundations, p. 98; © Bettmann/CORBIS, p. 99; AP Photo/Dennis Cook, p. 104; AP Photo/Scott Stewart, p. 108; AP Photo/Susan Ragan, p. 110; AP Photo/Ashland High School via the Ashland Daily Press, p. 112; © Mike Stewart/Sygma/CORBIS, p. 113; © David Paul Morris/Getty Images, p. 114; © Courtesy of Joe Gaskill, p. 116; © Brendan Smialowski/Getty Images, p. 118; © Kristoffer Tripplaar-Pool/Getty Images, p. 120.

Front cover: © JP Laffont/Sygma/CORBIS.

ABOUT THE AUTHOR

Betsy Kuhn's books for young readers include *The Force Born of Truth: Mohandas Gandhi and the Salt March*; *Prying Eyes: Privacy in the Twenty-first Century*; and *Angels of Mercy: The Army Nurses of World War II*. She lives in Maryland with her husband and twin sons.